LINKEDIN™
MARKETING
TECHNIQUES
FOR LAW AND
PROFESSIONAL
PRACTICES

MARC W. HALPERT

AMERICAN BAR ASSOCIATION
Solo, Small Firm and
General Practice Division

Cover design by Kelly Book/ABA Design

Printed in the United States of America.

21 20 19 18 17   5 4 3 2 1

ISBN: 978-1-63425-760-2
e-ISBN: 978-1-63425-761-9

Discounts are available for books ordered in bulk. Special consideration is given to state bars, CLE programs, and other bar-related organizations. Inquire at Book Publishing, ABA Publishing, American Bar Association, 321 N. Clark Street, Chicago, Illinois 60654-7598.

www.shopABA.org

Contents

Introduction. 1

Chapter 1: You Are a Brand. Yes Indeed. 7

Chapter 2: Your LinkedIn Profile: Think of It as a
Newspaper on a Newsstand 13

Chapter 3: Your Network Is Your Net Worth. Invest in It. 19

Chapter 4: Your Past, Present, and Future Rolled Into
Your Profile. 25

Chapter 5: Headshot Considerations That Work;
Look Approachable 30

Chapter 6: SEO Keywords in Your Profile; Using Searches. 35

Chapter 7: Your Headline Follows You Everywhere:
Better Make It Impressive 40

Chapter 8: Intro as Elevator Pitch; Add Specialties for
SEO Punch 44

Chapter 9: For Dual Professionals: Multi-Preneurship Tips. 51

Chapter 10: Sharing Updates: Blip on Others' Mental
Radar Screens. 55

Chapter 11: LinkedIn Long-Form Posts: Publish or Perish. 59

Chapter 12: Experience as Marketing: Your Past Makes
You Who You Are Today. 63

Chapter 13: Using Multimedia on Intro and Experience Sections. . . 67

Chapter 14: Showcasing Your Publications: Show Us
What You Write, All Right? 70

Chapter 15: Volunteer: Do Good 74

Chapter 16: Organizations You Belong to Can Add
Breadth to Your Profile 76

Chapter 17: Certifications: Show Them to Differentiate You 79

Chapter 18: Honors and Awards: Don't Be Shy. 81

Chapter 19: Skills and Endorsements: Making Sweet Lemonade. . . . 83

Chapter 20: Courses Taken/Teaching: Continuing
Education is a Two-Way Street. 91

Chapter 21: Formal Education as a Prerequisite; Alumni
Search Function 93

Chapter 22: Nonwork Interests: All Work and No Play Is Dull 96

Chapter 23: Call on Me, or Contact Me, OK? 98

Chapter 24: Halpert's 2% Rule on Recommendations:
Proceed Cautiously and Ethically 103

Chapter 25: Give Recommendations, Please. 108

Chapter 26: Effective LinkedIn Groups: Membership
and Participation 110

Chapter 27: Your Firm's LinkedIn Company Profile
Page: Not Your Website Please. .114

Chapter 28: LinkedIn Pulse: Communicate with Your
Personal Learning Network 117

Chapter 29: Who's Checking You Out; How to Use This
Information. 120

Chapter 30: How to Say "No Thanks" to a LinkedIn
Connection Request 123

Chapter 31: Navigating Your LinkedIn Home Page 126

Chapter 32: LinkedIn and Your Message: Specifics for
Your Industry 131

Chapter 33: The Mighty LinkedIn Help Center 133

Chapter 34: Considerations on Ways to Connect. 136

Chapter 35: Customize Your Public Profile and Be Amazing-Er . . .141

Chapter 36: LinkedIn's Mobile Apps: Be a Go-To Person 144

Chapter 37: Ethical Dos and Don'ts for Attorneys 148

Chapter 38: Pulling It All Together: The Proper Care
and Feeding of LinkedIn. 157

Chapter 39: Parting Thoughts to Make You a Greater
LinkedIn Success 160

Acknowledgments 163

Index. 165

Introduction

Did you ever think there was a book in you just waiting to be coaxed out? I did for years, and when I agreed with the American Bar Association (ABA) to write this book, I felt vindicated, peer recognized, and highly enabled.

For the past six years, teaching LinkedIn on my own, in my own way, I have shared a lot of quality time with other professionals. The makeup of the audiences kept aggregating around knowledge practitioners: consultants, attorneys, certified public accountants (CPAs) and finance pros, insurance producers, and financial planners, and so as not to leave anyone out, anyone selling tangible products or intangible intellectual services to those who need them. My work centers on helping others in these fields vying with a large number of competitors but who needed to answer central, self-defining questions posed to potential clients:

- "Why choose me?"
- "What unique values and skills can I provide you?"
- "How can I demonstrate my worth to you, in considering me?"

It's a hard decision for a consumer of professional services: how to decide whom to hire someone just like you (without a number of referrals by mutual trusted colleagues) or via a specific keyword search on Google, and/or on LinkedIn (if they even know they can do so).

Then on the short list of potential considerations, how does the consumer select *you*?

First they want to read about you. Before anyone will believe in you enough to place his or her future well-being in your hands and trust your professional guidance, no matter what you do, you must know yourself first and express your value to others. Muddy self-expression, or a résumé outlining your past, does not, and will not, win the game.

Why be like the others, who tell the minimum to get by on LinkedIn, only to further complain that they get nothing back from LinkedIn? No surprise about them. They are your competitors. Leave their myopia behind in the dust as you zoom by.

The key to making an impression on LinkedIn is clarity of message— stepping out from the noisy crowd to have others take notice of something unique you say and offer. Make it catchy, but do not expect anyone to fully absorb it the first couple of times.

Having said that, I am not limiting you to just explaining *what* you do and *who* you are, but I want you to go much further, deeper. Answering *what you do* and *who you do it for* does not deliver the emotional and intellectual impact that is implicit in higher levels of self-description:

- *Why* do you do what you do?
- With an extra layer, *how* do others confirm *why* you do what you do?

Better than *who* and *what* is *why* and *how*. Someone grasping your *why* takes repeating that theme in different places and in various ways or having others do it for you by opining *how* you accomplish your *why* as reinforcement.

Why and *how* work interchangeably when crafted well. The hard part is expressing it.

This overall approach is broadly influenced by Simon Sinek in his valued book *Start with Why* and accompanying blog and website.[1]

For the sake of clarity of voice and brevity of concept for my book, let's define *why* going forward as the acronym WYDWYD: *why you do what you do.*

And later in discussing endorsements and recommendations, we talk about HYDWYD (*how you do what you do*), as others echo your

---

[1] Simon Sinek, Start with Why: How Great Leaders Inspire Everyone to Take Action (2009); www.startwithwhy.com.

WYDWYD with their viewpoint and perspective upon your *why* from their own lens and experience with you.

While we are speaking about others saying *how*, I want you to know that you have absolute control over your *why* and over what others say and place on your LinkedIn profile, your *how*. Nothing is added to your LinkedIn profile without your consent, and you always have the absolute and final say over anything that brands you on LinkedIn.

In this book I show you how to properly manage and finesse your brand on LinkedIn. This self-monitoring is essential for everyone, but with special focus on attorneys and certain financial professionals who follow the stringent ethical and compliance guidelines in their industries.

Now let's put the focus back on *you*, the professional practitioner, who probably never sat through a personal marketing course in college or grad school. Marketing oneself is rarely offered in law schools today, amazingly. See the opinion blog post lamenting this situation at http://kevin.lexblog.com/2016/04/19/law-schools-slow-to-teach-social-media-and-blogging/.

If you did attend such a course, no matter how long or short a time ago, I assure you that marketing has changed a lot in the past years. And in the past year. And it's still changing.

Further, I suspect you are personally reluctant to talk about yourself in terms of WYDWYD, worried about sounding ego-centered, or have paralyzed yourself and your brand, unnerved at expressing your central branding attributes to potential clients, after years of finger-wagging and admonishment.

When I first started coaching clients, I saw a need to perfect my special sauce, attuned to professional people I train, coach, lecture, and cajole; any of my LinkedIn concepts is designed to help them get out of their own way, past the parents and teachers who stymied them, to express to potential clients WYDWYD and get others to add HYDWYD, all told, to surpass their competition.

That's a lot of emotional branding for a professional to adapt at once. And for most, it comes out reluctantly, slowly, and irregularly. Eventually with some discussion, it becomes more fluid, and with my editing, better refined. The "a-ha" moment occurs when the professional actually enjoys self-defining with words, concepts, actions, anecdotes, and graphics—an editable mélange of experience painted in a self-actuating way.

Over time I kept meeting professional practitioners who held more than one terminal degree or multiple professional certificate designations: attorneys with Certified Financial Planner (CFP) certification, CPAs who were trained in the law, financiers with either, or both a CPA and law degree.

And I encountered others operating more than one business at a time, as I do myself, so I attracted other owners of multiple businesses in diverse industries, needing to mentally and emotionally tie the business interests together for others to understand them as the de facto head of the firms. Their/my quandary: how can you show others the *why* behind the diversity of professional interests just as clearly as the owner personally sees his or her combined missions?

I sat through dozens of seminars, read the books, scanned the e-zine articles, and met personally with coaches, trainers, speakers, and authors. I knew that other how-to books, cheat sheets, and quick seminars on "four major social media platforms and how to use them for marketing, taught in an hour" were dated, or cursory, and certainly too generalized to a low common denominator of understanding. You have seen them advertised—too many social media generalizations crammed into a single session, probably best left to one social media platform per session, or better yet, a strategically designed session attuned to the needs of just one professional practice. Yet there remains the whole audience of underserved dual designation holders who need to learn personal LinkedIn marketing techniques. There is still no other place to get that.

After a discussion over breakfast in New York City in late summer 2015, the editors at the ABA were open to the concept of my book. I was pleased. I have a living laboratory of business pros in my daily work to observe and analyze the best ways to help them. This book serves to solve the issues I find in that research.

Is this the book you need?

Can you write beautiful, professional work on complex topics but when coerced to self-define your value proposition and personal brand, you hem and haw? Has your career brought together vital skills that others do not possess and that remain valued in our economy? Are you a dual professional designation holder? Do you consider yourself a multi-preneur?

Then, you have much to gain from what I am about to write about. But you must agree, "I shall willingly talk about myself on LinkedIn." Repeat that.

As we explore the LinkedIn marketing tips and techniques that have proven successful for my professional practitioner clients (single- and dual-designation holders alike) and have been perfected over the past six years, I encourage you to take style notes and translate these ideas through your own lens and voice, in your own writing style, to your own professional personality. Use your unique ways to answer WYDWYD with contributed examples of HYDWYD. Experiment and tweak these concepts continuously, appealing to your clientele and practitioners in ancillary areas of expertise to build more business.

I always say everyone I encounter is amazing in his or her own way, but how do you stand out? You have to look *amazing-er!*

That's the purpose of this book. If you ever sat through one of my classes or webinars, you know I shoot straight from the hip—honest and direct. And I try to make it fun. OK, not every joke is a rib splitter. This book is no different—me speaking to you, short chapters on digestible topics to keep you focused, and some themes repeated in different ways in different chapters.

Each chapter in this book is designed to offer you, in a very short reading duration, some practicable self-marketing techniques to consider. I want you to implement the tips in your own voice and style of communication. No two of you will be alike.

This is not a "plug-and-play-LinkedIn" book or a "how-to-do-it-in-three-minutes-a-day" type of guidebook. I try to keep the charts and "how-to-do-this" to a minimum. Besides, I wouldn't author one of those how-to-books: first, we already have too many of them, and second, with Microsoft acquiring LinkedIn, the whole book would otherwise be obsolete before printing. That would still be true even if there were no Microsoft acquisition, given the way LinkedIn routinely changes its formats, as was recently introduced in the newest user interface on desktop screens. And everything I am showing you to brand yourself in this book is available to you, without taking a subscription to LinkedIn.

Yes, I know you can figure out LinkedIn yourself (this book, by the way, is *not* for dummies). Mostly, if LinkedIn changes a section, the graphic look may change but the end result does not, so that's a good thing for all of us. That means the conceptual need for that LinkedIn section remains eternal—it's the look and feel that were polished.

Likewise, the self-branding concepts I bring you in this book are time tested and timeless. They may serve you in many other endeavors over the years and are certainly not confined to a certain version of LinkedIn, or just to LinkedIn itself. Think broadly and creatively. You know your audience.

I hope you have fun and discover new ways to express WYDWYD, and tell the professional world your values and skills. You need to.

Let's get started.

Chapter 1

You Are a Brand. Yes Indeed.

Marketing is how we come across in images, gestures, and language and other ways that are believable, in the varied ways we convey ourselves, repeatedly over time, to influence and spur the customer/client to act, buy, and return again to get our help. (My definition.)

Wait! Talk about ourselves?

As was lamented above, we were all taught by parents, teachers, and other influencers *not to* talk about ourselves, as it makes us appear ego-centered, stuffy, conceited, and self-impressed. These negative adjectives we were warned about come easily from memory.

And no one ever taught you in law school or in your MBA program that you *had to* market yourself, and/or the firm you work in.

OK, let's leave old-fashioned notions behind and relate personal brand marketing to today's market environment: *start talking about yourself.*

"People I've been referred to always check my LinkedIn profile and are then aware of my background, talents and skills before we even make first contact. When we do finally communicate, they're eager to talk to me because they already know that I'm unique and am very good at what I do. Plus, they might have even vetted me.

By putting all my accomplishments on LinkedIn, my Profile serves as my intro letter/resume/testimonial/PR person.

I assume that others preview me because that's what I do with them."

—**Gene Braunstein, Comedy facelift.com LLC, Norwalk, CT https://www.linkedin.com/in/genebraunstein**

Your twenty-five-year-old competitor is. You need to as well, drawing on the quality of time spent in the trenches and the wealth of experience gained, with quality, not in excess, not about what an expert you are and how you mastered every topic you practice, but rather, in light of the knowledge you can impart to others to show them best how to do better, to help them.

Pay it forward, right? See the movie by the same name again, and this time when you see it think of its overarching message in light of today's business social media, LinkedIn in particular: how you can give back to your connection network without expectation of receiving anything in return, and when you do receive back, it is served to you in bucketfuls.

So it is with LinkedIn: you have a special view, talent, message, or value proposition that other business people need (there you go marketing yourself); you can show them the way, but you need to use the most efficient ways to widely and effectively share your refined brand message as a professional practitioner to help others. The market (however you define it) needs to see you continuously in action—posting selected words and images more than a few times, varying your themes, and adapting the timing and technical aspects of your unique work and its past successes—before any of your message will begin to sink in. You telling your "why"; others adding their "how" about your "why."

LinkedIn readers are evaluating you. Perhaps they will read most or all of your profile and then begin to believe in you, while you show WYDWYD, reinforced by the admiration from recommenders and endorsers. The result, as your brand conveys about you, should be a call to action—a phone call or an email to you to further assess if considering you as the right person might solve their need:

- They found you or your firm in a general LinkedIn search (ah, the finesse if you know how to achieve this result).
- A colleague verbally referred you to someone and they found your LinkedIn personal profile or company profile (again, success, if they were motivated by your relationship with the mutual colleague and your LinkedIn profile message was compelling enough for them to go the next step and contact you).
- A mutual connection recommended or endorsed a skill you possess, based on firsthand observation that reinforces your

message, made that much more believable when from a trusted colleague.

- They came across a Post you wrote, or an article you shared with your connection base, causing them to want to know more about you, the curator or the commentator, given your perspective.

"When I am working to express on LinkedIn what I do and why I do it, I find that I do two things. First, I read the summaries of people I know and listen for their voices in their written words; next, I try to write as I talk. I appreciate authenticity in others and try to live it myself."

—Jane Beddall, M.A., J.D.,
Dovetail Resolutions, LLC,
New Haven, CT https://www.
linkedin.com/in/janebeddall

- They recognize your stature as a fellow LinkedIn Group member, and they value the experience and insight you bring to the discussion at hand.
- You reached out to them and introduced yourself intelligently, offering context to help them identify the opportunity, as a candidate worthy of consideration for connection.

Each or any combination of these can lead to eventual collaboration, right?

But you have to earn the connection. You must first carefully craft your profile and use it as a lever to back up being considered as a memorable, valued connection. Then your reader is interested, he or she will connect with you, continue to read what you share, and immediately remember you for an appropriate situation utilizing your skills, making you top of mind when an opportunity suitable for you comes forth. Admiration and referral come to those who work at it and are deserving—that demonstrates confidence in you.

This makes you sound like a brand name, right? That's where I am going: *you are a brand*.

A quote from Lois Geller[2] that I like to share in my educational sessions about "you as a brand" is

---

[2] Lois Geller, *Why a Brand Matters*, Forbes (May 23, 2012), https://www.forbes.com/sites/loisgeller/2012/05/23/a-brand-is-a-specialized.

"If you're going to develop your brand, the last thing you want to do is follow the beaten path. You want to head down your own road. Your brand has to plant itself in the hearts and minds (especially hearts) of prospects and customers."

You must be searchable, accessible, believable, valuable, and memorable—and not only on an intellectual level. That cerebral part's important, don't get me wrong. But it's just not the only way to resonate. Everyone has a different way of being impressed enough to act. Consider some new ways to market your brand:

- Be repeatedly interesting and thus encourage others to follow you.
- Be relevant and adaptable to changes in your field(s) so your viewpoint stays current.
- Be reliable and evaluative as a spokesperson as the issues change and evolve.
- Be a thought leader to add clarity to complex issues.
- Be vocal, videoed, podcasted, published in any way you can communicate in your market.
- Be visible frequently enough to be memorable, and offer quality insights each time.
- Be emotionally impressive. Yes, emotion plays a part in all sales, too.

Scientists reassemble facts. Artists reformulate emotion. Entrepreneurial, hungry professional practitioners need to demonstrate their expertise levels in the client's buying experience by knitting emotion to the facts, using rich images and nuance to add as veneer to the black-and-white. We buy with more than our brain.

It's the "heart" mentioned in Geller's article that sways a client/customer/consumer. Remember that business people are very highly educated, motivated, spending consumers. But as consumers, they make fast decisions with their hearts and minds.

Solve their need, relieve their pain. Often the pain is an emotion with an obvious (to you) objective solution that you bring to light. Speak to the audience on many planes so they preselect your solution to resolve their challenge at hand and recognize you over the rest of the other practitioners who could just as easily jump in. Based on something you did, said, hinted at, or were referred for, it made you different in a remarkable way.

> "I was hesitant and nervous to talk about myself on LinkedIn. Then I realized that if I focus more on experiences and lessons learned as a way to promote myself and my business, I could showcase myself and my company as a thought leader within our industry without sounding self-centered or conceited. This approach has proven to be very successful in networking with other potential franchise owners throughout the country."
> —**Josh Cohen, Founder & CEO, Junkluggers, Stamford, CT https://www.linkedin.com/ in/josh-cohen-5597988**

There it is, the artful science (scientific art?) of self-branding—facts intermingled with emotion and pain relieved by you practicing your craft.

Talking about yourself well in verbal or electronic words in marketing terms is powerful stuff. It's not always what you say; it's how you say it, at the same time. The reader is hunting, but not for long. Grab the reader's attention and keep it. Incent them to act. Make them want to return for more satisfaction.

But you have to get going. Some professionals, when considering their LinkedIn profile renovation, relish starting, launch by jumping in, and learn about themselves in the process. Some quickly decelerate and then freeze. Others bristle with revulsion at even starting and relegate it to the bottom of the procrastinator's heap. Most others get clogged somewhere in the middle—unsure, moving sideways.

Beware lethargy; this is serious stuff. It must be planned before being started. It must be thoughtfully evaluated, presented honestly, and show introspection. It must have a straight-line trajectory; this should take time and probably several drafts.

No one else can say it like you can. And no one else should, so channel your best authentic voice and point of view. Let it seep. Don't rush it. Your LinkedIn profile and personal brand marketing will coalesce around your themes and values, slowly and in due course. Six years later and my profile is not perfected; I am still tweaking mine bit by bit. It's pure admission of WYDWYD, in my own words and voice.

Let me add four more observations that will make you think about LinkedIn, your point of view, and self-marketing, perhaps in a new way:

- Only you can place material on your LinkedIn profile, and only you can approve others' comments on your LinkedIn profile. That means you have absolute control over your brand on LinkedIn. I urge you to use this empowering tool to build your professional brand organically, originally, and continuously.

- Deny the nonprofessional chatter arising from politics, word games, number puzzles, and kitten and puppy pictures that creep into LinkedIn, making it feel more like Facebook some days. Keep the direction you want to go, or face the embarrassment of a peer calling you down for deviation from professionalism.

- Your changes appear on your LinkedIn profile in real time. There is no delay time or interpretation by a web designer between you and your online profile. If your profile is brilliant, you alone should be proud. If a change is needed to update your trajectory in your career, you can make it immediately. If your profile is stale, you let it get that way.

- And finally, if there's a typo or grammar error, a bad link, an old or lame recommendation, an off-base comment, or an endorsement by someone not knowing your skill, you allowed it. The bottom line is that you own your profile, and you need to protect it: This is a reflection on you and all you stand for. The immediacy of it all can be exhilarating. It's your brand.

We start with presuming LinkedIn is *the* marketing platform for you and your professional practice. You deal with other professionals, B2B. You need to recall that every professional is a consumer (per Lois Geller's quote). Then, what you do on a phone call or in an email reply to someone who selected you from LinkedIn is completely up to you, but what you say to the client on the phone must be in sync with and reinforce the persona they bought into in your LinkedIn profile.

Your LinkedIn personal profile has to be perfect—or as close as you can make it.

Wait. Don't jump in head first and start revamping your LinkedIn profile yet. Take one step at a time.

In Chapter 2, let's take a high-level look at the LinkedIn profile.

Chapter 2

Your LinkedIn Profile: Think of It as a Newspaper on a Newsstand

Busy, time crunched, attention deprived. We all suffer from sensory overload.

But once we have our mental aim set on procuring a product/service/advisor, we propel ourselves to use any and all tools to find the best from among the many and select the finalists for the A List. Your goal is to be on that short list.

That's a lot of great businesspeople clamoring for attention in a limited market—a giant searchable LinkedIn network of professionals offering personal advice from their expertise area, and asking for the same, 24×7×366, a database growing by over two people per second every day, globally.[3]

So before we concentrate on you, let's pause to take a look at your impressions and images of *others*. How do you prioritize your work and allocate attention to those who need you?

As an example, each morning you come to the office and open your email. Whoosh—the barrage of emails flies in, and each one needs to be handled, in a way that resonates and makes sense to the addressee. No two are alike. How do you prioritize your responses?

---

[3] https://press.linkedin.com/about-linkedin.

Is it by order of the higher-paying clients? By the issue that needs immediate attention above all others at this moment? By the seniority or longevity of the writer as your client?

You start to think: which first, then how to reply, based on the urgency and the addressee; you subconsciously arrange your thoughts and key in a message that speaks specifically to the reader.

And think of the people who flash across your screen all day—who call, who email, who text, who message, who touch you in some way. Some mental images you have of them are visual and some not, some are collegial, some are even adversarial, some are fact based, and others are emotionally driven. Yet in every instance that you communicate with them, you assign an order to answer them, and then you pick your words, phrases, and paragraphs to convey your message in a way that will mean the most to each of them.

Or you ignore what appears to be uninteresting, worthless messaging, and/or spam.

What about the nagging need to market, to plan, and to attract future clients—despite the distractions of today's fire drills—and to backfill the pipeline when existing clients dry up, business scales back or is lost to a competitor, or the client's urgent case is resolved?

The past, present, and future can work at cross-purposes. Time is finite. Attention spans are short.

Now flip this around: think of how others see *you*. Using the mirror, do they see you or think of you first, fast, immediately, and do they perceive you exactly as you want them to?

To them, you want to be easily thought of, your advice perceived as needed, on a path with them to impress and assuage with every touch. It's a process. All impressions you have developed over time come with considerable effort.

You are continuously cultivating the image of WYDWYD *(why you do what you do)*, using a commonly accessible platform so all can see you, anytime, anywhere.

Have you expressed that "why" on LinkedIn exactly as you wish to be seen, to be recognized for your specialty, remembered, and then immediately searchable, and better yet, approachable?

Consider that LinkedIn is the leading platform that each savvy business pro uses multiple times a day as a brand marketing forum and a related search engine. It allows you to market yourself with the cultivated image and unique voice you need to project your personal and company profile pages.

And they had all better be really good.

The LinkedIn platform, however, can get mighty crowded if you are buried amid the competition with other run-of-the-mill profiles, listing themselves, stuck in time, posing as a generic brand.

I said "listing themselves." Yes, many wrongly use LinkedIn as a glorified curriculum vitae (CV), copying and pasting data that is often more than a few years old into the electronic real estate called the LinkedIn personal profile. They take no time to keep it current or take the effort to make it interesting, compelling, relevant, and state-of-the-art.

> "On LinkedIn, you should connect smartly, i.e., with people you really know, or who you can be helpful to and vice versa, but think long term. Like anything else, you get what you put in, so it's advisable to have a strong profile, join groups (but participate!), make periodic status updates, or comments for your best exposure, offering to help others.
>
> Go live/offline/make a phone call as soon as you can since in business, you need to get real; most people have some degree of email, text, and related fatigue."
>
> **—Robert Fligel, CPA, RF Resources Partner Search | M&A | Succession Planning, New York City, https://www.linkedin.com/in/robtfligelrfresources**

Thus, the majority of profiles are boring, backward-looking recitations like the "About Us" page on the website, or worse—a résumé where the historical data was lifted from in the first place.

Thinking of your competitors' presences on LinkedIn, you can hope their LinkedIn profiles are boring. Here's the bad news for you: *they likely will not stay that way.*

And readers' attention spans are shortening. Most readers casually scan for phrases and keywords, thus capturing their attention wherever they land on your profile is essential. And they may read top-down or bottom-up or even jump all around. Thus, every section has to be really good. The bottom line is that the total image you convey must be greater than the sum of the parts. You need to stand out, section by section and in entirety.

One way to do this is to free yourself from the {bullet point} {past tense verb} {accomplishment} résumé paradigm.

Now is the time to go the extra mile and work on your profile to make it robust and stand apart from the competitors—in your own

"Since focusing more effort on updating my LinkedIn profile and background information, people have found me which has provided some interesting opportunities. This was due to the managing editor doing a LinkedIn search on independent financial advisory firms focusing on certain market demographics. A trade publication ran a major article on my firm giving us some media attention."
—**Harvey Spira, Founding Principal, Hyperion Wealth Advisors, New York City http://linkedin.com/in/harveyspira**

words, with your own story. Write as if you are speaking directly to the reader. "I" is how we speak about ourselves, as if you were conversing with them. I don't know about you, but I do not speak in bullet points.

To illustrate the point of this chapter, let's use a time-tested model of standing out from the noise and distraction: the newsstand. It worked for centuries, and it still works.

Your LinkedIn profile is like the latest newspaper edition on the global newsstand. People rush by, but no one even stops to buy a newspaper on a newsstand unless something jumps out at them. It has to be compelling to get the buyer to stop, scan, pick it up, and purchase, and there are always quite a few papers to choose from at any one time. You need to capture attention with a pithy headline, a graphic, and an intriguing lead paragraph that introduces the story, with quality writing, before they want to read further to absorb the details presented later in the article. This is your personal input, with others adding color and weight to your facts.

Like the newsstand, LinkedIn profiles are like business speed dating, a mating game that has no real rules, based initially on capturing emotional attention and visual appeal with facts and a snappy elevator pitch thrown in.

That means employing attractive wording and colorful graphics, just to be noticed. That also requires an opening paragraph to capture the reader's attention and entice him or her to read more in the profile. Pictures demonstrating much more than words can convey are always useful to make a point better.

People who might consider you as a trusted advisor are impressionable, yet their attention changes quickly. They may have a usual financial advisor they are leaving, or have been referred to you as an insurance specialist, or are attracted to your specific architectural expertise, and you will not even know they looked at your LinkedIn profile until it's too late.

You had better be immediately interesting—never boring, never a résumé on electrons. You must speak to them in words on a screen as if you are conversing in person. Impersonality is no longer believed to be efficient. The personal touch of word choice and tone in an impersonal world is more treasured. Their new attention to you and your offering(s) needs to be captivating, so they want to learn more about you.

Your goal is to have them read as far down your profile as possible, as they quickly scroll down. Some recruiters read from the bottom up, they tell me. They may stop to absorb a concept or idea you profess. Hopefully they feel the urgency to springboard from your profile and contact you. From there, it's in your hands.

Let's switch scenarios. The phone rings. The caller may be reviewing your LinkedIn profile as you converse. You should be reviewing theirs at the same time. In doing so, find the common threads that tie you to the caller with the hints on his or her LinkedIn profile and fashion your conversation skills around them:

- "I see you went to {X University}. I have a close colleague who also studied the Classics as you did and it seems you are close in years. Perhaps you know {Y}?" *or*
- "{Same question but substitute a firm in which you and the caller cut your teeth early in your careers}" *or*
- "You and I share fifteen connections. How do you know {X, Y, and Z}? In fact, I regularly eat lunch with Y like we did the other day. Next time, join us" *or*
- "I read your article in {A} a few weeks ago and thought it was right on target. Perhaps we can discuss that {case/situation/philosophy/method} when we meet" *or*
- "You are in a LinkedIn Group with me. Do you get the same benefit from conversing in the Group that I do?"

LinkedIn lets you uncover new clues. You must then knit in these uncovered common threads we share to make phone calls and face-to-face meetings much more valuable and memorable.

LinkedIn provides a research tool in one place that you can access immediately on your screen (or via its many apps on your smartphone or tablet), and it becomes a focus of your next unexpected phone call.

"LinkedIn has changed the way in which we identify and recruit people to talk to for our research projects, giving me the ability to reach anyone and ask for their participation. The credibility I get through LinkedIn has made it possible to provide insights we never would have gotten.

My LinkedIn profile has opened the door to connect with people that others may not be able to get in touch with and it has made the difference in a lot of the projects we have worked on."

—**Rob Goldberg, Partner, MIDIOR Consulting, Cambridge, MA https://www.linkedin.com/in/ robgoldberg**

Once near strangers at the onset of the call, you hang up with a new colleague sharing a growing connection—personal touches in a too-often impersonal world.

Now you must realize that these personal touches make recalling your name or expertise much more memorable a week, or a month, later as the mental connectivity is easier to pull up. You want to be easily remembered in every possible, positive way.

OK, now you have to work.

Open your LinkedIn personal profile. Take a hard objective look.

Have you provided the backstory, the data, and the color that a caller or casual reader can utilize to digest your value proposition and then *want* to contact you, meet you, and/or engage you?

If you can't answer that objectively, ask a friend, significant other, colleague, or someone who will be brutally honest with you: "does this LinkedIn profile depict me well, as I want others to know me professionally, as you see me? And since you are being honest and know me so well, are there areas that I need to beef up, reword, delete, update, add new sections, etc.?"

This is about telling WYDWYD, and you have now made a start in rethinking how you brand market yourself and your firm. Now that I have made the case to renovate (or completely gut, if necessary) your LinkedIn personal profile, let's talk about your audience(s).

After we talk about your audience, we will take each section, one by one, to explore together how you can get the most marketing traction out of each. At the end we will compile all of them, where the whole profile conveys so much more than the sum of the parts.

Chapter 3

Your Network Is Your Net Worth. Invest in It.

Interpersonal business networking relationships, as evolved over the past decades, are predicated on making each touchpoint as fruitful as possible. We recognize we can't do it all alone. Though our attention spans have contracted, we still need to concentrate on the core tenets of growing our business: revenues, expenses, cash flow, expertise, network relationships, and marketing. Each has many experts offering to help us do better.

Surrounding ourselves with other effective go-to colleagues is essential to our success. I teach my clients and workshop attendees that it's the interactions and interrelationships that we routinely cultivate that make us more valuable colleagues, a two-way street.

We tune out the people we meet who seem insincere and unmotivated; we are attracted to sharp businesspeople with dynamism and imagination. Still, new relationships are entered into quickly—sometimes too quickly.

> "I do have a technique that's been working for me ... because I've added 200 new contacts. I make it a habit to make six connections a day. Now that might not be six new connection requests. It might be to have a follow-up conversation or to ask someone to introduce me but I try to touch LinkedIn each day ... and sometimes I do more and other days I do less, but if I can convert a conversation to a connection, I'm on the way to a possible opportunity or qualified prospect and a possible sale!"
> —**Jeanne Boyer Roy, VP Sales, ValueSelling Associates, Essex, CT** https://www.linkedin.com /in/jeannebroy

Often we never eyeball the other person in the equation. In the case of my esteemed collaborator, Geoff Geertsen: he is a very close business colleague two time zones away, though we have never personally met after doing business eleven years, and we collaborate daily as energetic and trusted partners. You probably have some of these relationships, too.

Before I connect to someone on LinkedIn, I take the time to vet the person, get to know him or her, and cultivate that person with investments of energy and effort, in scarce time. In sum, it's a contradiction that we have to embrace—making immediate impressions about people for long-term, quality relationships.

LinkedIn is the marketplace where the world's professional talent comes together, virtually, to reinforce our interpersonal connectivity within the communication efficiency of the Internet.

You have to "work" the crowd on LinkedIn. LinkedIn massages our network and encircles new colleagues, but it's a practiced art. Pay it forward; help others with their need to learn from you and help them meet other effective businesspeople through you.

The end result is rich dividends of an enhanced net worth. Your trusted network will appreciate that you care. Colleagues will admire your efforts and warmly refer you as a result. That's why I called my company "connect2collaborate." When you connect and collaborate by keeping in touch far more than annual holiday greetings, you share great learning material routinely, and you tie great people together to share knowledge, then you are at the top of each other's minds. Value and practice these fundamentals and you will succeed.

This is why my network is my net worth. Your network is your net worth. No two networks/net worths are equally valued. In my portfolio of financial assets, some will turn into cash cows (those that return the most in the investment), some may totally surprise me, suddenly bursting with promise, while others may lag with only a prayer to pop later. Yes there will be duds to be flushed out when possible. The portfolio will be an assembled group of diversified and reliable holdings.

Your networking net worth is the wealth of your experience and the good people who admire you for it, tap into you to benefit themselves, and refer you to their net worth holdings—that is, their colleagues, who they know can benefit from your value.

I want to be clear about one thing: your "cash cow" best connections are the ones you nurture. They believe in you. You work to help them, and they help you back. You know who they are. They may come and go. When needed, one only needs to stick out a hand and ask for or provide support (a two-way street).

Your role is to grow a group of trusted, valued connections into an entourage, as my colleague Leslie Grossman defines them in her book *Link Out* that:

> *gives you great advice, ensures that you receive valuable intro-*
> *ductions and referrals, and surrounds you with a group of*
> *influential people who offer their support throughout your*
> *career. In order to create these trusted relationships and estab-*
> *lish a long-lasting entourage, your role is to do the same for*
> *them. Each member helps each other and then pays it forward.*[4]

The entourage needs continual polish with your ideas, warmth, wit, suggestions, and questions to make them think with you, such that the by-product is the expanding elasticity of you in their new thoughts.

This entourage connection concept is not a passive activity; it takes work. They value you for your actions, thoughts, and leadership. All these take energy and the confidence to step out from the crowd to make the extra effort. Meet in person with them, following Leslie's advice, a strong complement to great ways to activate the honest and real input you can solicit from your entourage by electronically linking in as well.

Many still think we can *only* network in the old-fashioned, passive way yet pay minimal lip service to the present-day need to have a LinkedIn presence, and then grumble "it's" just not resulting in business knocking at the door. The "it" that is not working for you may be your social media presence; in business, your LinkedIn profile. "It" is no longer the twentieth-century method of print advertisement solely in obsolescent media like newsprint, yellow pages, trade directories, working the phone, monthly chamber of commerce meetings—these are no longer the only ways to gather new business followers.

---

[4] Leslie Grossman, Linked Out: How to Turn Your Network into a Chain of Lasting Connections (2013), 17–18.

I ask: living in the past, what magic are you expecting? There's a new "it," a whole new ballgame that includes, to a *very* large extent, LinkedIn as the predominant business social media. For some solo practitioners, small firms, professional practices, organizations, nonprofits, and even companies, social media is the only medium they use. And for some of those, LinkedIn is how they do "it" best, with feet in other marketing areas as well.

So get over your resistance. Embrace "it," and use the tools available to grasp business and self-promote.

Do you see others actively engaged effectively in participatory, run-with-the-ball social media networking? They succeed in new ways. You can, too. LinkedIn allows you to augment these new methods and virtually contact serious businesspeople well outside your physical location and comfort zone.

LinkedIn is the new power tool in your professional marketing toolbox. Get comfortable with the concept, and get serious about talking about WYDWYD, and stand out from the crowd.

To initiate the self-definition process, I use a few stream-of-consciousness questions, recorded for playback later, as my clients tell me:

- What role do you play?
- What do people think about you?
- What do they actually say about you?
- What do you want people to know about you that is not clear on your LinkedIn profile?
- Why should I hire you as a consultant/supplier/employee/resource?
- What are you curious about, and how do you use it in your business?
- *And most importantly, WYDWYD?*

For some, the responses come rapid-fire. This becomes the basis of the weekly homework assignment I give my clients to begin to weave their answers into a richer narrative on their revised LinkedIn profile. For others, it doesn't come easily, and they struggle to put words around their answers. With my help, we continually rewrite and improve what they want to convey as they journey along in business. It takes work.

Why? Because we are all changing, evolving, and growing. I know I am. You are. And you need to tell others why, how, and where this is leading you. If you don't, no one else will, or it might be your competitor, and then you will not be pleased.

Only you sense your world is changing, even if you do not want to let on that you're changing. You may be evaluating a new start-up phase or may be privately contemplating a lateral move. Or it's back to basics as a retrenchment. No one else needs to know—we are moving too fast. But if you are changing, you have to tell us when it is right. Until then, everything before the change also has to be articulately described in terms of *why*.

> "My goal is to present my personal mission, passion, expertise, and experience in a way that viewers can quickly determine what I do and whether I might be able to help them succeed. In a pitch meeting I have the benefit of asking questions and uncovering challenges and opportunities, but the end goal is the same—figuring out together if I can help. I try to use the full range of profile tools (e.g., rich media, lifting up specific skills, emphasizing accomplishments, causes I care about, etc.) to be as helpful to my profile viewers as possible."
> —Larry Eason, Consultant, DotOrgPower, Los Angeles, CA https://www.linkedin.com /in/larryeason

LinkedIn is evolving as well, and before you exhale and say, "I just don't have enough time to do this," or "I need an assured return on investment to make this worthwhile," or "I will wait for the next iteration of LinkedIn so I can start then," place yourself back a few decades and think of how you said something similar when you started learning word processing or spreadsheets. Back then, you put in the time as an investment so that today you can pump out a finished document or financial analysis with relative ease and efficiency. You got over the early-on resistance to learn how to best use the tool. Yes, it took work. Now it is second nature, and you know the tricks to complete an assignment a lot faster, with experience.

Start by carefully evaluating LinkedIn personal profiles of people you respect: those who tell you about themselves in a polished, professional manner, and convey their value proposition extremely well. What concepts and images do they transmit to you that make you want to engage them in a conversation, perhaps leading to a business association?

In your eyes, *why* do they do what they do? Do you admire that others augmented the *why* with their recommendations and endorsements of *how*? Take style pointers from them, start a fresh, new word processing document, and start to tell your own story in your style and self-expression. Be professional but still sound approachable. Leave the acronyms and jargon out, as not everyone who reads your profile wants to wade through the terminology. Remember, the reader's attention span is short. Confusing or frustrating the reader will make him or her click away, forever lost as a potential business partner, and thus you are no longer under consideration.

Now you are starting to talk about yourself as a contributor to the net worth of your entourage—them to yours. Rest assured, it takes effort. Rewards will come.

But where does all the narrative you need to say actually go in the LinkedIn profile? How do you tell it well from a perspective that leads a reader to perceive where you came from, where you are now, and where you want to go? Unsurprisingly, I have those ideas for you.

Chapter 4

Your Past, Present, and Future Rolled Into Your Profile

Too often, copy-pasting a résumé to LinkedIn is seen as the easy way out of not having the time or creative capability of expressing your self-brand of WYDWYD.

Consider the ubiquitous résumé: backward looking, past-tense verbs, bullet points, superficial, only valued when it is required for a specific job search. It reports the bulleted factoids of a candidate's career, looking back into the past, obliquely offering a tenuous glimpse into the candidate's present-day situation while his or her future is briefly scanned for that new position. No matter how many years' experience, it is constrained to two pages and lacks pronouns. It lacks color. It is not conversational. It is dull, drab, boring.

How can anyone expect it to capture the wealth of decades of work maturity, quality of your experience, acquired skills, industry thought leadership, refined observations, and honed personal values, all together making you the person you are today? How is one to determine from this paperwork what you can offer in the future? It can't help you, as it is.

Indeed, many recruiters admit they stopped actually reading résumés years ago—today I am told résumés are machine scanned for keywords. Then a list is produced containing the names of those with the most mentions of the required keywords, and candidates likely for review. Your résumé and the others are mechanically selected as competitors.

Where do recruiters and human resources executives review you further? On LinkedIn, of course! It's where they pay for a subscription to fill in all the huge gaps and read between the lines to evaluate you from the short list for a phone interview, using LinkedIn as a more detailed analysis tool to assess you as a likely fit, with the right experience or creativity or skills needed to fill the position.

You're not a job seeker, you say? Take the recruiter example and let's stretch it a bit: delete "recruiter" and insert "prospective business client" as the LinkedIn user instead; they need services either from you or from a competing firm.

Where else can a prospective client connect your values, skills, written observations, rich experience, and client *hows* and prequalify you to be considered a vendor, advisor, or partner, all in one place? LinkedIn, of course.

Now is the best time to free your LinkedIn profile from the shackles of frozen résumé time. Your LinkedIn profile changes dynamically with every new concept you act on, every new breaking development in your field you absorb and respond to, with every profile update you make. And since only you can make an update, the onus is on you. There is no web designer to wait for; you alone make all changes, in real time. Again, you have to want to, and must think about, "working" it to keep your profile real and up to the minute.

In doing so, use your rich and valuable past experience to show what mental and emotional values you bring with you today, and how those will drive your future as a colleague.

Are you perceived as ascending? Or have you taken a parallel track to a new career place by embarking on an encore career—taking a sidestep from the traditional legal firm to a CPA firm, becoming a wealth advisor after years as a teacher, stepping into a corporate finance position, landing in a support industry to the law, or going outside the traditional pathways completely? Why did you choose that? How can you provide insight to the reader to show the true benefits from challenging yourself in an uncharted industry or field that drew on your previous skills?

A well-developed LinkedIn profile allows you to express WYDWYD *today*, based on the skills and character you have developed in your *past*, and aim for the rosy optimism of what the *future* will bring you and your client.

Slow down for a few minutes, or as long as it takes, and re-read your profile: does it tell us *why you do what you do? Past? Present? Future?* No? Then you are behind in telling your own story, so now is as good as any time to start, and you'd better get busy, before someone interprets your past for you. Your profile will be only as good as you can tell WYDWYD yourself.

Now, reversing the process, if you need a CV for any reason, such as an exhibit to a proposal, you can use your LinkedIn profile to form its basis. Create a CV from your LinkedIn profile, using LinkedIn's own internal tool. To do this, click the three horizontal dots to the right of your picture on your Profile page and select Save to PDF.

Marc W. Halpert

LinkedIn coach & group trainer helping you look amazing-er | cashflow strategist to firms & nonprofits using e-payments

marchalpert@gmail.com

Summary

I help you get "unstuck." I specialize in 1) coaching and training to look "amazing-er" on LinkedIn and optimize it for your business and 2) providing you the tools for faster, smarter e-payments to improve your cash flow. Read how:

#LinkedIn Coaching and Training
I use LinkedIn as the power tool in my marketing toolbox; a focal point for branding myself and my businesses. I'll show you how to do this too.

If you're an entrepreneur, attorney, accountant, insurance exec, nonprofit pro, HR, sales, consultant, seeking a job, or between positions: it's all about branding yourself well. I'll coach you to jumpstart the referral pipeline.

My work is customized: 1-to-1 coaching, group training sessions at corporations, professional service firms, small companies, membership organizations, nonprofits--yes, for anyone who wants to learn how to REALLY use LinkedIn!

See www.connect2collaborate.com for daily LinkedIn nuggets.

#Faster, Smarter e-Payments Improve Your Cash Flow
I show your business (my brand Your Best Interest) or nonprofit organization (my other brand (e-giving) how to accelerate its incoming cash flow with:
• credit/debit card and/or electronic check debit payments
• one-time and/or recurring payments
• a custom secure shopping cart that looks exactly like your website.

Your goal: freer, faster cash flow into your bank account. See www.yourbestinterestonline.com and www.e-givingonline.com.

##So, You Might Ask...How Are My Business Interests Intertwined?
I am meet amazing professionals who are stuck. They need my e-payment solutions, and they become my LinkedIn clients; many of my LinkedIn connections also use my payments services.

The end result—in my case it's a twenty-seven-page long PDF document of my LinkedIn profile (from which the first page is shown). This can be produced using these instructions: https://help.linkedin.com/app/answers/detail/a_id/4281/kw/PDF. From here you can revise it according to your needs.

The discussion so far in this chapter presupposes you have rewritten your profile to be deeper, richer, and more compelling (in my words, "amazing-er") than the competition's, and certainly far better than any bulletized résumé!

Do you need help to be sure you have edited and captured your best profile possible? Ask friends and colleagues in your entourage to read and critique for their opinions. Ask them: does this capsulize me well? Did I leave anything out? Can I say something better?

A brief but very important aside—before you start making changes to your profile, be sensitive to your connections' perceptions and inboxes. Do not allow LinkedIn to send them each a notification each time you make a change to each section. We all have received notification that someone changed a small detail in a current job, and it seems they took a new job when in fact they had not. The congratulations pour in. Uh oh. Wrong impression!

To keep this from happening to you, open "Sharing Profile Edits" from your Settings and Privacy section, then click the Privacy tab at the top, and look for a switch that looks like:

By default it is on Yes. Turn it to No. Make your multiple changes on your profile. When completed and saved on LinkedIn, turn it back to Yes. From then on, all changes you make and articles you share on your profile will be communicated to all your connections.

Think carefully about if and when to tell others you made changes to your profile. This preserves your image and respectability among peers. Be aware of the control you have over what and how you disseminate your news on LinkedIn.

OK, let's start with marketing techniques for each section, from the top, of your LinkedIn profile.

The guided tour of the best LinkedIn profile you can develop begins now.

Chapter 5

Headshot Considerations That Work; Look Approachable

Probably like me, you've resisted sitting for a new headshot. "Too time consuming." "I really look the same as a few years ago, and besides, my needs for a headshot never change." "No one hires me based on what I look like." "I don't want anyone to know what I look like."

Uh, not quite.

Your brand depends on a high-resolution photo that makes you look professional, approachable, recognizable, and friendly.

Find a professional photographer who specializes in photos of business professionals, look at his or her online portfolio, admire the best, co-opt the style you want to convey in your headshot, and venture into the "shoot" with the mindset it is an investment in your self-branding. The results can be useful in many circumstances that you may not even foresee today: a brochure, a website, publicity for upcoming speaking engagements, and even, as I found, on a book cover!

Frontward looking, your photo is the brand of you, visually, and with the nonverbal impact that you want to convey. Products and services are designed to be visually appealing. We buy with our eyes and hearts (as Lois Geller mentioned in that quote from her *Forbes* article in Chapter 1), and the first impact is a glance at your headshot. When you upload a square headshot to LinkedIn, center it within the circle so it appears best to you and your reader.

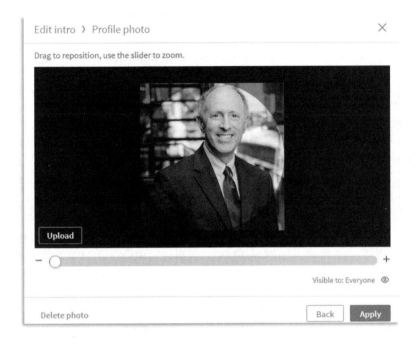

From fifty-one initial proof photos in my shoot to choose from, I consulted my most trusted entourage of advisors, and narrowed to nine then five then three. I chose two different backgrounds. My talented photographer sent me three versions of each final shot. I have narrowed it down to one photo, which I submitted to LinkedIn, and it was then properly sized and formatted to become my LinkedIn headshot.

The rest of the proofs I received from the shoot will be, or have already been, used to refresh my other marketing materials. So you see, the headshot investment can serve your social media and other marketing needs.

So a word to wise men and women: get your headshot shoulder-to-top-of-head large enough to make your face easily seen elsewhere on LinkedIn. That was easy.

There are some limits on the headshot photo file you can use.[5] Generally you can upload:

_____

[5] See LinkedIn's Help Center at https://help.linkedin.com/app/answers/detail/a_id/1615.

- JPG, GIF, or PNG files;
- up to 8 MB maximum;
- The ideal pixel size for your photo is 400 × 400.

What should you wear? If you follow my "head-to-shoulders" advice, the concern over wearing a suit or business casual attire means less if the bottom of your headshot is shoulder level. The viewer is thus looking at your face, not judging how formal or informal an outfit you wore. There, easy fix. No more worry about formal or not.

In my most recent headshot, I chose to wear a tie and blazer as a compromise between the varieties of dress codes I encounter. One side of the internal argument I held with myself favored a suit (for most of my law and financial clientele, although this is changing rapidly), and the other side leaned toward an open-collared dress shirt (like the consultants, entrepreneurs, and nonprofits I meet with frequently).

Ultimately I chose the blazer/tie because I generally find that dressing that way works best when I speak to groups or to a small company. I always ask the person who hired me what is appropriate. Often business casual is fine. If in doubt, as my wife counsels me, dress up one notch.

By the way, stay away from dressing in fine-stripe shirts and tiny plaids that can make you dizzying on photos. Most photographers provide website guidance on how to dress ahead of the photo shoot. Read the online ideas from a few of them.

Don't forget the photo's background also portrays a message. I used a blurred-out outdoor scene behind me for urban emphasis, suggested by my photographer as we stood on his fire escape. I can alternate between this and a white-background headshot that is more formal.

Attorneys can use a background of shelves of legal books or the front of a courthouse; finance professionals can try backgrounds with their clients' capital projects. Consultants can appear from their desk to be looking up, smiling, and open to a question. CPA photos I have liked show them at their desks, crunching numbers. Marketing experts can use a photo of themselves in action at a client or with a product launch. Public speakers have many hand gestures and poses to choose from as the conference venue usually sends in a photographer to capture the candid moments of the event for post-publicity and next year's advance public relations. Just be sure we can easily and clearly see your entire face.

Finally, get comfortable with your photographer, laugh, smile a lot, relax, and be yourself. You will then look and feel approachable in your headshots.

As I did, ask your photographer and entourage to help you select the best of the headshots for the look and impression you want tied to your mental brand. Remember, we all have a mental image of what we *think* we look like. Allow others to assist you in this choice so what you really look like comes across on your LinkedIn profile. This is the immediate impact to a reader learning WYDWYD.

I collect the best (and the worst) headshots I run across, and include them in presentations. It is astonishing what is out there on LinkedIn! As I always say, the *very worst* headshot photo I ever saw on LinkedIn was . . . . . *no photo at all*. But some others in my collection come close.

Here are a few last tips:

- White backgrounds are still fine (Given the changes with the 2017 user interface, a white background makes your profile almost completely white at the top so a color background to your headshot shows you off so much better! I advise you not to wear a white shirt in front of a white backdrop or your head will appear to be floating! Yes, I have seen that.)
- I always advise against a background that is blue-gray stormy and seems threatening to launch a tornado. I think we had enough of those in grade school.
- Use a professional to shoot your photo. Cropping out your spouse and colleagues from a candid photo taken on a smartphone at a company holiday party looks less than classy.
- Your company logo is not suitable as your headshot. Similarly, no landscapes, words, or animals as the photo.
- No matter how much you love your kids or pets, they do not belong on the headshot with you, unless you own a pet store or operate a day-care center. But you probably do not.
- If you change your hair color or dramatically alter your haircut, get a new headshot.

Keep your brand image fresh, friendly, and approachable. See, visibly looking great and professional on LinkedIn isn't rocket science after all.

While we are on the topic of adding a photo, take the time to add a wide background photo above your headshot to make your profile more visually interesting. Think about a shelf of legal texts, a courthouse, you in action in a mosaic of photos across the width of the page (as I did).

However you can show your work in a quick glimpse, the reader is drawn in to want to read further. For the specs on a banner, see https://www.linkedin.com/help/linkedin/answer/49960?query=background%20photo.

Chapter 6

SEO Keywords in Your Profile; Using Searches

Getting mentally ready to rewrite your profile requires some planning and forethought: your goal is not only to concentrate on what others will see in your value proposition but also to be found in a LinkedIn search. The best profiles are those that not only tell WYDWYD but also allow others to find you, or people just like you, using specific and deliberately chosen search keywords.

For example, more efficient profiles are found when performing a search using terms such as "D&O insurance pro," "sweepstakes IP attorney," "multinational corporate banker," and "forensic accountant," than when using general terms such as "insurance," "lawyer," "finance," and "CPA."

I want you to be in that search result.

LinkedIn is an immense database (as of this writing over 467 million members) used by the global business community to search for and contact others who are needed for any number of business reasons.

The dilemma is, how do you simultaneously make the most of the desire to express yourself and the need to be found?

First, are you familiar with SEO (search engine optimization)? Ask your web designer what SEO keywords and metatags he or she used in your website. You use the search engines to find something efficiently; likewise, SEO can help us find you easily, too.

Web designers are adept at using the Google AdWords Keyword Tool, and you can learn about that topic at https://adwords.google.com/KeywordPlanner#search.none. Think of LinkedIn search as a subset of the various search engine queries, but in this case, it aims at business professionals and their primary needs—what LinkedIn provides best.

So before you start the arduous task of writing and rewriting a lot of new material, you need to make a few lists of the possible SEO keywords others might use to find you. Put yourself in the seat of someone looking for you: what terms would they think to use in a search that will result in your profile being found on the list—and even better, in the top five on that list?

LinkedIn automatically stack-ranks the reported search results by keyword density and then by your first-level connections (those you are connected to formally), then second-level connections (those your first-level connections know but you are not connected to), then mutual LinkedIn Group connections, and then all the rest (third level). Given the variability in who is connected to whom, no two people will ever get the same search results on LinkedIn.

Compile the final, select set of best keywords and then incorporate these keywords into your rewriting of these main four LinkedIn profile sections:

- Headline
- Intro (formerly called Summary)
- Experience
- (strongly influenced by your) Skills

Although LinkedIn will never reveal its search algorithm, my fellow experts believe that these four sections are especially sensitive to keyword search right now. This list can (and will) change. As stated above, you need to write your entire profile, section by section, very well, now, and for the future iterations of LinkedIn itself and changes to its search functionality.

What's most important here is that you are more likely to receive a direct business inquiry resulting from a keyword search if someone reads your richly presented narrative in your profile, and/or knows you directly or indirectly through a trusted colleague. Why? We prefer those whom we can rely on (or know others who do) versus those we do not know at all. But you have to be in the search results to start with. And then you have to make the researcher fall in "like" with your profile enough to contact you as a potential business colleague.

So to drive home the point, adding to the burning desire to be "found" in LinkedIn searches that many business pros are performing these days, you need to not only eloquently differentiate yourself from the competition but also use specific and general SEO terms that will make the LinkedIn search engine point to you.

A word of caution—being findable in a LinkedIn keyword search is your goal, but don't go overboard. Don't deliberately "stuff" these sections with such densely packed SEO keyword phrases while aiming to ace the electronic search that bore or confound the human reader. A numb human mind triggers a finger click on a mouse to change from you to someone else's LinkedIn profile. Click, and they never look back. And that's a forever-lost opportunity.

A few general paragraphs are helpful to best use LinkedIn's search for your own needs.

A simple search is common when you seek something concrete: some component of a profile of a person (name, location, job title, etc.). Or perhaps you are seeking a specific company or a few companies. The white search box at the top left of any page on LinkedIn can bring you to the possible matches for searching names of people, job titles, company names, groups, universities, keywords embedded in long-form Posts or keywords to find mail in in a LinkedIn Inbox.

Filter People by   Reset

Connections   ^

☑ 1st   ☐ 2nd   ☐ 3rd+

Locations   ⌄

Current companies   ⌄

Past companies   ⌄

Industries   ⌄

Profile language   ⌄

Nonprofit interests   ⌄

Schools   ⌄

Want to better focus your search?

    Function
    Years of experience
    +9 others

Try Premium for free

This is where I start when I need to look up something fast or simple: a single-variable search.

This is where I test my search capabilities to find others in a complex search, especially in the four above-referenced sections that are SEO sensitive. I have learned to employ Boolean search terms to make the results more useful and efficient. For more information on this, the

link from the LinkedIn Help Center is https://www.linkedin.com/help/
linkedin/answer/75814?query=boolean.

So being findable takes some research, and being memorable takes
some creativity, both for practical reasons. As stated, I suspect that the
sections in which SEO matters for LinkedIn search results will change
over time. This is an evolving structure and will morph as time and user
needs change. However, learning to master it now will only help you in
the future as it develops.

Chapter 7

Your Headline Follows You Everywhere: Better Make It Impressive

When teaching classes or coaching clients, I advise them that one of the most challenging of all the sections on LinkedIn, which absolutely must be written very well, is the Headline.

You are distilling decades of experience into fewer characters than a tweet, to entice the casual attention-starved reader to read further along in your profile. Using the earlier metaphor, you are appearing on the global newsstand that LinkedIn created. People "passing by" your LinkedIn profile will stop to consider reading about you only if you have a compelling Headline that makes them want to read more.

A LinkedIn Headline is only 120 characters, including spaces. Anything more than 120 and your excess characters fall into the void. Thus, condensing WYDWYD, after decades of work, into such a small space is really challenging. If it doesn't require you to develop multiple iterations trying to say the same thing more economically, you haven't tried hard enough.

Most people take the easy route and paste their title and company name like "Partner at XYZ, PC" or worse, "Owner, Acme Financial Associates." But do these two Headlines make someone stop and say to him- or herself, "Hmmm. Sounds interesting. I want to read more about this person" and act to do so? I doubt it.

These shortcut Headlines contain no value proposition, no life, no interest factor, no brand of you. Nothing more than a factoid is conveyed. Nothing to make the reader think you could actually help him or her. In our attention-deficit world, that's not getting you seriously considered, much less even noticed, as a candidate for that case, as a contender for a new job, as a consultant on that assignment, or as a manager of that big project.

Rather, revise the {title} at {company} Headline and think hard when you create each iteration; use your word processor to keep these draft Headline versions, and cut and paste the best of each into a single one. Edit it as often as you have a change to convey in your initial contact with a stranger-to-be-colleague, and eventually you will come up with a clear and concise Headline like the one below.

What makes a Headline great? Let's dissect one from a well-regarded connection who "aced" her Headline:

"Helping to add confidence to client financial decisions |
Expanding our team of career-minded financial associates"

First, it's 114 characters including spaces (I let my word processor count that), just under the 120-character maximum. Could she have added six more characters and done any better? I doubt it.

This shows the proper use of capitalization, without abbreviations, jargon, or industrial lingo (and there is plenty in the insurance field!).

Next, see how she divided two separate aspects of her work using the "|"? (That's the key found above the enter key on any keyboard when you use the shift and press it.) It helps the mind and eye of the reader see that there are two distinct thoughts being presented and uses minimal characters. I advise using it in a Headline to express how you are doing two things simultaneously; if you have two or more aspects of your work, the "|" key will point your reader's attention to the impression you work in different fields or areas, a handy character-saving convention to express who you really are in terms of the different ways your professional time and work efforts are spent.

First aspect of her Headline: she uses the verb *helping*, which shows her ability to offer her skills to the needs of her client. She *adds confidence* in financial decisions in a market that can be confusing and risky. *Client financial decisions* contains the search keywords in the LinkedIn search engine that will help her be found more readily using one or more of the words in that phrase.

Second aspect of her Headline: she is a recruiter of financial salespeople for her company, *expanding* (which is a richer verb than "seeking" or "hiring," so again, the suggestion to use rich action words) a *team* (yes an overused term, but knowing her, it's sincere and real). *Career-minded* is a rich adjective—think about the active images she is conjuring in the minds of the reader. *Financial associates* is an SEO term that job seekers would use in the LinkedIn search engine for sourcing employment opportunities.

For other great action verbs, see https://www.themuse.com/advice/185-powerful-verbs-that-will-make-your-resume-awesome.

So you see, she has accomplished a lot in 114 characters. In one quick glance, you know what field of work she is in, her desire to help, that collaborative passion she brings, what client qualities she conveys, and the two aspects she performs in her professional services firm.

The need to be economical in keystrokes often encourages creativity, but be sure the reader can identify the terms you use; the inclination to use jargon or acronyms here to save spaces will only confuse, unless they are commonly recognized. Hint: use certification acronyms after your name to conserve more space in the Headline for self-description. Another hint: using MBA after your name looks pretentious. It's not a certification; CPA and CFP are.

The Headline makes you crave more information, gets more eyes on your profile, starting with the Headline at the top and driving the interested reader downward toward the bottom, or as far as they can get. That's the aim.

Years ago, a coaching client called me from her car, after she pulled over to the side of the road exclaiming she had been driving along and (eureka!) the Headline came to her subconsciously and she just wrote it down. And it was a gem! She was highly unusual in that it came to her all at once and required little sharpening. Do not expect that to happen to you, although if your inspiration comes at inopportune times, be sure to write it down for later use. Some clients tell me it comes while asleep. Really.

One morning while driving to my appointment, I heard a radio ad for the Nathan's Famous International Hot Dog Eating Contest on July 4 on Coney Island in New York City. They renamed the hot dog eaters "gustatory competitors," which got me chuckling and also pondering how creativity can be used to call yourself something unique and add clarity to your persona all in your LinkedIn Headline.

I've called myself a multi-preneur, which is not my own original term, but one I have pinned on myself. I like that; it is clear, creative, and keeps me top of mind. In past iterations of my Headline, I have called myself a "LinkedIn Trainer and Evangelist," which conjures up an image of a passionate advocate with certain zeal to those who need to be convinced and, thus, changed, in some way.

Colorful/memorable? I try to be. You can, too. I encourage you to work on that Headline slowly and publish it on your profile when you are content it perfectly reflects WYDWYD in so few characters. This is not easy to write; it is perhaps the most rewarding part of writing on LinkedIn when you ace it.

I suggest you rethink your Headline as the preamble to the rest of your profile, the Intro coming next. Reusing the right terms and phrases in the next, more expansive profile section can further crystallize your image in the minds of your readers.

Chapter 8

Intro as Elevator Pitch; Add Specialties for SEO Punch

As I mentioned, your LinkedIn profile Headline is well worth the considerable time and effort to perfect. In 120 characters or less, it makes the reader want to know more, a process to help him or her determine if your profile suits the need. It sets the tone and stage for the rest of your profile.

In each subsequent section we explore in this book, your job is to nudge the reader to continue reading down, down to the end of the profile, or as far as you can manage the reader to go. You started the curiosity at the profile Headline, next urge the reader to learn more about your overall persona, in more words, in lockstep with, and every bit as enticing as, the Headline, further laid out in your Intro.

Using the same newsstand metaphor as in Chapter 2, the Intro is you delivering a readable elevator pitch, but it's a short ride. Attention is highest early on, so optimize this brief opportunity. It's you speaking to the reader as you are saying, "Here's what I want you to know, why I do what I do, all rolled up into a short précis of my life's work, past, present, and future."

No, don't belabor the reader here with details of various present and past jobs (save that for the jobs in your Experience section). The reader has not "bought" into you quite yet.

The Intro is where you can go further to pique the interest that started in the Headline. There are overriding themes in your career, and valuable insights you possess, all of which are refined by experiences, adaptable to the need of the boss/client/customer at the time. This is the chance to tell about your overall values and character (even how to properly spell your name), as you continue to whet the reader's appetite.

There is more you want to tell—the values, character, and breadth of what you do daily, and why you do it that way, as if you are saying "Profile reader: keep reading as I expand my narrative and you see my virtues."

Then clearly lay out in complete sentences the unique credentials, skills, and characteristics you layer into your overall business practice, what you bring to the proverbial table, as you describe yourself in your Intro.

"Why you?" is not just the beginning of WYDWYD; it allows you to expand beyond simplistic questions of who and what to expand by describing the why these attributes (the DWYD) comprise your business self.

> "Because the Intro section is searchable for keywords, lawyers and other professionals should include relevant search terms in this section of their profiles. That includes not only the words they believe people looking for someone like them would use, but also common misspellings of their names, particularly for those who have unusual or difficult first or last names. Thus, as my last name is spelled Abeshouse, I have included the following line in the Intro section of my profile:
> *(Note: My last name often is misspelled as Abehouse or Abeshaus or Aleshouse or Alehouse.)"*
> **—Atty. David Abeshouse, Law Office of David J. Abeshouse, B2B Dispute Resolution, Uniondale, NY https://www.linkedin.com/in/abeshouse**

- What past experiential knowledge did you gain, that you presently bring to the conversation, to win the confidence of the person reading your profile?
- How do your core beliefs and personality further add to your achievements, to your attractiveness as a business partner, advisor, confidant, trustee, representative?
- Adapt the input from your entourage here to tell more deeply about yourself using powerful, confident statements: "I see unusual opportunities that others do not and monetize them . . . ," "I am uniquely experienced in . . . ," "I am complimented for my . . . ," and "My clients tell me they appreciate my . . ." (all within your industry compliance and ethics constraints).

Yes, there is a fine line between self-branding and boasting. Beware of language that makes you sound self-absorbed; invest in well-constructed narrative that resonates you as self-reliant, in terms of how others rely on you. Get over the inner resistance to self-express your unique value proposition, while being the consummate professional and volunteering your insight. Once again, the right keywords interspersed in rich sentences throughout the Intro help your search results on LinkedIn.

Focus: Whose Intro Is It Anyway?

A client emailed me two drafts of her LinkedIn profile Intro to look over and give my opinions to help her choose which version I thought was most useful.

Neither, I replied by email. I insisted on a phone call so I could verbally explain that she confused the company profile with her personal profile. This will only confuse the reader, too. I asked her, why tout the firm she works for in her *personal* profile Intro?

To make it better, she needs to use the personal profile intro to speak about *herself*: her business journey from her past experience to who she is today and where she expects to go. In her case, she is not the firm. She may be strongly influenced by it, proud of it, but in her drafts of the Intro she was not telling me *why her*; instead, she was telling *why the company*. She needed to spend more time and effort making us "buy into" her personally as a professional services provider.

Please, as you write your Intro, don't confuse the two.

If her current passion is about working for that firm, it's expected that she mention her role in the firm's successes in her Experience section (see Chapter 12), but points in her Headline and Intro must be made relevant to *her* own personal value proposition.

My advice as her LinkedIn coach was to let the firm she works for talk about why the company versus the competition. This is best done in the company profile page (more on this in Chapter 27).

One of the most prevalent misconceptions of professionals in their LinkedIn profiles, especially solo and small-firm practitioners, is to entangle and confuse the personal Intro with the company profile summary. Even if you are the sole member of the firm, write about yourself here in the Intro and characterize your firm in the company profile. You can find the fine line.

And here's another tip to get the reader's interest piqued enough to click down from the first lines of your Intro. Your profile only shows the top two lines of your Intro. That's approximately 232 characters, including spaces until it cuts off with an ellipsis (. . .) and the reader is expected to click to open the rest of it.

Marc W. Halpert

LinkedIn coach & group trainer helping you look amazing-er | cashflow strategist to firms & nonprofits using e-payments

connect2collaborate (division of Your Best Interest LLC) • The George Washington University - School of Business
Greater New York City Area • 500+ &

I help you get "unstuck." I specialize in 1) coaching and training to look "amazing-er" on LinkedIn and optimize it for your business and 2) providing you the tools for faster, smarter e-payments to improve your cash flow. Read how:...

See more ∨

But will they open it? The importance of these 232 characters cannot be stressed enough to capture their attention about how you can help them and encourage them to want to open the rest of it, thus your being able to fully explain yourself in the Intro. That means you need a "call to action" so they will click to see the whole Intro:

Marc W. Halpert

LinkedIn coach & group trainer helping you look amazing-er | cashflow strategist to firms & nonprofits using e-payments

connect2collaborate (division of Your Best Interest LLC) • The George Washington University - School of Business
Greater New York City Area • 500+ &

I help you get "unstuck." I specialize in 1) coaching and training to look "amazing-er" on LinkedIn and optimize it for your business and 2) providing you the tools for faster, smarter e-payments to improve your cash flow. Read how:

►LinkedIn Coaching and Training
I use LinkedIn as the power tool in my marketing toolbox; a focal point for branding myself and my businesses. I'll show you how to do this too.

If you're an entrepreneur, attorney, accountant, insurance exec, nonprofit pro, HR, sales, consultant, seeking a job, or between positions: it's all about branding yourself well. I'll coach you to jumpstart the referral pipeline.

My work is customized: 1-to-1 coaching, group training sessions at corporations, professional service firms, small companies, membership organizations, nonprofits--yes, for anyone who wants to learn how to REALLY use LinkedIn!

See www.connect2collaborate.com for daily LinkedIn nuggets.

►Faster, Smarter e-Payments Improve Your Cash Flow
I show your business (my brand Your Best Interest) or nonprofit organization (my other brand (e-giving) how to accelerate its incoming cash flow with:
• credit/debit card and/or electronic check debit payments
• one-time and/or recurring payments
• a custom secure shopping cart that looks exactly like your website.

"Build it and they will come. Over the years I have developed a dynamic presence with my LinkedIn profile. I have added articles and videos on the topic of business communication to my profile and I publish a post at least one time per week. It is quite exciting when I receive an email that begins with the line "I saw your profile on LinkedIn and would like to learn more about your services."

—Jayne Latz, Corporate Speech Solutions, New York City, https://www.linkedin.com/in/jaynelatz

Focus: Eyes and Ears on the Prize

Video is the medium that *should* provide the greatest memorable benefit for you, used effectively; it provides the best mental recall of your passion and value proposition to your connections. If not already doing so, you should start leveraging video to showcase yourself in today's business networking via social media.

LinkedIn makes uploading your video persona to your profile really fast and makes it accessible. Other technologies make the act of video recording really easy. You just have to make a few short compelling videos, with different messages and topics—this is no easy task at first.

But once practiced and finalized, you can add a general video introduction (like a video elevator pitch) in your Intro and/or add a separate brief video showcasing a product, service, or skill you want to call out for specific attention to a job in your Experience section, so video works well in two places on LinkedIn. But note the difference in topical thrust of the video (overall general character of you in the Intro; then tied to a specific job in your career in the Experience section), and the choice needs to be made carefully for placement in either your Intro or Experience sections. As of now, video cannot be added to any other profile sections.

Be sure you have combined these components to make a successful video:

- Find a savvy, talented videographer (like you did with your great headshot photographer) with whom you are comfortable. Ask for referrals. Styles and experience vary widely; techniques and equipment play important factors as well.

- Shoot it indoors and/or outdoors. It's your decision, and recall that backgrounds add value. Beware distracting ambient noise, so shoot at the quietest time of day for the outdoor venue or filter the sound well.
- Make it an economical, yet clear, verbal message (attention spans are normally limited to thirty seconds), so how you word the message should be tight and pointed.
- Practice your message delivery and make sure it is energetically spoken (try it in front of a mirror). Practice and practice again.
- Emphasize your spoken points with hand gestures, vocal intonation, timing, and keyword titles on the screen as you speak (ask your professional video producer).

Supply an easy way to contact you as the video wraps up.

Think: it's like a TV ad, but for less than forty-five seconds. Well, thirty is better. Think: how can you be most memorable early on, using your face, voice, intonation, background, and direct message?

Note the backgrounds. With the right videographer, it's painless, creative, and actually fun.

The first frame is from a general video elevator speech that I posted to my LinkedIn Intro. Below that is a frame from a video about how I train groups in companies and firms that appear in my Experience section as a LinkedIn coach.

As I say in my "live" sessions, get out of your own way and talk about yourself, *both* in the written word and reinforced by your verbal points on video.

Be professional, be yourself, and be approachable. It's your brand they are buying.

Video gets opened, seen, and best of all, recalled.

Chapter 9

For Dual Professionals: Multi-Preneurship Tips

Beyond evangelizing on LinkedIn, another aim that I have in writing this book for the American Bar Association is to assist those with

- Dual designations (attorneys with a CPA, other law school-trained professionals who no longer practice the law but work in other industries, etc.)
- Other "multi-preneurs" like me and so many whom I come across, for whom life's journey has them engaged in multiple entrepreneurial areas of interest, thus operating more than one business at a time.

The challenge is: how do you clearly and concisely show the world WYDWYD when it's challenging enough to express it for just one business, let alone two, or more?

Well, you start with a common denominator, some sort of entwining concept, and you write your LinkedIn profile and its component sections reinforcing the threads; in turn, you make it easier for the reader to understand that two or more industries or businesses or degrees set you apart in some special way as a unique business colleague, yet you are one whole individual from whom they can rely, hire, seek advice, refer, etc., based on your unique skill sets and viewpoints—not the multiple industries, per se, but one person, and one story to tell about yourself.

No one is able to tell how to reconcile the two or more parts of your professional brain better than you. So make your case cohesive and clear, despite the inner suspicion others have that no one can master more than one complicated business pursuit, and (gasp!) even do it well. We can.

But we have to work a bit harder to tell WYDWYD. Simply telling "who" and "what" you do in two sectors will never suffice. "Why" you do these things and "how" you pull them off are essential.

Start with the Headline: pack those 120 spaces with the two or more concepts that define your multi-preneurship. If you like, use a colon to introduce a concept and semicolon to divide them up. Various past iterations of my multi-preneurial LinkedIn profile Headlines appear below:

> ### Marc W. Halpert
> Multipreneur: LinkedIn 1to1 coach, group trainer, speaker; e-payment pro to nonprofits & business; I exceed expectations

> ### Marc W. Halpert
> Multipreneur: I coach/train you to look amazing-ER on LinkedIn; I help firms & nonprofits maximize cashflow w/epayments

> ### Marc W. Halpert
> Multipreneur: LinkedIn branding & positioning trainer/evangelist | e-payment pro accelerating nonprofit and biz cashflow

> ### Marc W. Halpert
> LinkedIn coach & group trainer helping you look amazing-er | cashflow strategist to firms & nonprofits using e-payments

In the past I also found it effective to use the "|" (that key above your keyboard Enter button) to divide the segments according to my work areas, as shown in the third example above. It allows two different thoughts in a place where spaces are very dear. Recall how in Chapter 7 my colleague did such a fine job of using the "|" in relating two different roles in her Headline.

The multi-preneur's Intro section can be divided into two (or more) subsections reflecting each of your business exploits. Using arrow symbols, I draw attention to my subsections, after starting with a statement to say I have two interests. Then, using a single arrow symbol, I delve into each WYDWYD, then finally wrap up with dual arrows to reinforce the common thread and tagline. Use whatever symbol works for your personality and needs, just be sure there is a separation so the reader knows to look for more information in your Intro displaying your multi-preneurship.

The writing style of my Intro is much like how I speak in my sales efforts in person, and in writing to my blog readers, and so it should reflect my tone and personality to the reader of my LinkedIn Profile. My hope is to energize him or her to contact me. I want to create the essence of "why me," especially with two seemingly unrelated business interests.

Your expression and style may differ. Emulating the profiles of others with multiple business interests who you think have a great profile can be used for style notes as you interpret their creative energy and help you impress others: why you, with your own multi-preneurship reasons, in your LinkedIn Intro and other sections as well. Be yourself.

Ask others in your entourage to review and offer edits and suggestions. Throughout, keep it aligned with your personality. Fully explain WYDWYD as many times as you have different business interests.

Combine them in a tightly wrapped package to finalize the thoughts, so the reader sees your points of view once more. You must be realistic: this may be confusing to some. Make it clear, in your own voice, easily absorbed by all.

Chapter 10

Sharing Updates: Blip on Others' Mental Radar Screens

Curating great material is always an expedient way to be recognized as a consistent contributor and thought leader. What goes around comes around, as I see it. Share quality, a lot!

This means going beyond merely attaching an article someone else wrote; rather, tell us in your words why you shared the article. There's that "why" again. Go beyond appending Twitter hashtags. There are two ways: updating your status, uploading a photo or curating an article, and publishing a long-form Post, found toward the top of your Home Page.

Let's take each one at a time.

Update your status. Make this a habit.

1. Frequently enrich your network with quality material you have chosen that will make you even more memorable and appreciated. Use targeted language to tell your audiences what you are doing professionally and offer insightful comments why they will benefit from the article you recommend.

"Opine weekly. This also contributed to (gaining a) social media–derived client, since at first the prospect liked one of my updates (with lifestyle information), and then checked out my profile. He sent me a connect request, having seen the breadth of my network (600+ at the time). He's now a client."
—**Susan Glusica,** *Susan D. Glusica, President & CEO Libelle Prosperity Solutions LLC, Pine Bush, NY* **https://www.linkedin. com/in/susanglusica**

The most common questions I get when I speak on this topic are: why constantly share with your connections? Does anyone care what I am doing or reading? Who needs more reading material?

Here are the best reasons: do this regularly so they know you are out there always creating value, and they can find you again quickly at your next shared contribution. That's another positive mental image they get of you, a reward for you offering helpful, relevant material, appearing on their radar screen often. They will appreciate your giving without receiving (again, the pay-it-forward comments I spoke of before). If they respect you, they will savor what you recommend.

Another question I get is how often should you share valuable information? It depends. Feed the virtual personal learning network that surrounds you, as often as you have quality to add to the conversation. There is no magic number of comments per day/week/month. If you are somewhat quiet by nature, you may feel it best to offer material once in a while, or as often as you see something that will help a certain individual or group of people. If you are an outgoing sharer, do so as often as is consistent with your generous personality, but gauge the quality of the material and effectiveness of the results. Too much can be overlooked as spam.

2. Upload a photo: share a graphic in these formats: JPG, GIF, or PNG files. LinkedIn does a pretty good job of resizing the photo for you. Then tell us why you shared it.

   Here's a real-life story. A savvy LinkedIn user called, saying he needed to know how to share an infographic (PDF) to show his connections on LinkedIn. His dilemma is that it's not really an update (like an article), it's not really a photo, and it's certainly not a Post. "What should I do?" he asked me. Well, reasoning this out loud with him, I said that I believe a PDF of an infographic is closer to a photo than anything else you can choose among the three choices we get to choose from, so I advised him to upload it as a photo. The PDF was on his hard drive, and his update with the PDF uploaded as a photo looked fine, was admired, and was appreciated widely in his connection group. So I add PDFs to the usable file formats in this upload-a-photo section.

3. Add an article: as stated above, append the URL of the article and please tell us why you like it enough to have curated it for us. Or tell us (professionally) where you disagree.

Word to the wise sharer—too much noise, or low-quality shares, or obvious self-advertising is a curse. I have a connection who told me where he ate breakfast, lunch, and dinner on his daily postings; to me this is like static on a cell phone call—annoying—and I tended to ignore his updates routinely, even if they were possibly (rarely) interesting.

Another tip is to use updates as a lever to stay in touch with some outliers, distant prospects, and former clients; offer them relevant insights in your field of expertise, volunteer professional observations, and link online material that you come across.

For example, as I write this, it's Sunday morning, and I just shared an article in today's *New York Times* about the charitable deduction and potential changes to the tax code, which I sent as an update to some esteemed out-of–New-York-City metro non-profit connections and also to certain of my LinkedIn Groups (more on this in Chapter 26) with my commentary on why this article is relevant.

What I want to happen to you is what I love to be told: "wow. I really liked that article you posted a few weeks ago on {subject} and passed it on to five of my favorite clients. Thanks!" What's going on here? I am having a positive effect on the people I nurture. They will look out for my other LinkedIn updates going forward; I am a larger blip on their radar. They thought enough of my material to share it with clients. I feel good knowing I am giving back to my network (read: enriching my net worth), and they feel comfortable referring my material to their valued connections.

Pay it forward indeed! That's what you want to strive for in sharing material and commentary on LinkedIn.

In the next chapter, we look into the other option for updates (it deserves its own chapter) as we explore branding yourself among peers by publishing a Post.

Chapter 11

LinkedIn Long-Form Posts: Publish or Perish

Publish or perish in entrepreneurship is the same as in academia. We benefit from the world's newest perspectives, opinions, expressions, observations, and experiences—all contributing to colleagues what we can relate to in our own business experience or, better, learn from others.

The third way to share is a powerful one: publish a Post—an original essay on a topic we can all relate to or benefit (think: magazine article).

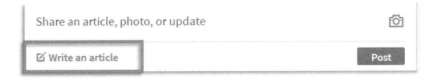

With a banner graphic and catchy title that makes others want to stop and read it (that newsstand metaphor), keep it at 200 to 750 words of material (although there seems to be no maximum word cap on Posts) to make them want to read it all the way through, even though they suffer from short attention. Cap it off with a call to action, your brief bio, and contact details. Finish by choosing a few keywords preceded by a hashtag (#) that will help others search for your Post by topic or keyword. Choose your hashtagged keywords carefully.

"We prepare and post blogs (on an almost daily basis) on cutting-edge legal developments/decisions in our areas of practice. We do this for multiple reasons:

1) It demonstrates that we have our "finger on the pulse" of the respective industry that we are blogging on;

2) It forces us to remain abreast on the current status of the law; and

3) It increases our SEO on the particular topic—hopefully leading to prospective client calls/emails for legal assistance on the topic."
—**Atty. David O. Klein, Klein Moynihan Turco LLP, New York City https://www.linkedin.com/in/davidoklein**

You've seen colleagues post these essays; perhaps you have, too. Here you can give others your unique point of view and send it globally through LinkedIn to be commented upon, quoted, liked, and its URL shared. It's your differentiator, your value, your competitive edge in an all-too-noisy world, so being able to chime in clearly and as frequently as you have something great to share is a virtue! If your Post is really popular, LinkedIn may add it to a subject channel on Pulse, the news service home of Posts, for even greater visibility. Score!

Posts are a service from LinkedIn to facilitate communication and thought leadership to LinkedIn readers, globally. You can be sure you will gain attention and a following from those who find your material regularly useful and relevant. I repeat: regularly, useful, relevant—ah, quality! And Posts tend to float around globally for a few months after release—the timelessness of thoughts.

Quoted above, an attorney in New York City sends out a near daily (!) Post to opine on recent cases and judgements surrounding his intellectual property practice. He smartly presumes that reading his daily Posts will spread his reputation among peers, clients, prospects, and others who believe his topic is timely. By following his Posts you can get a good overview of the depth of his expertise.

If you have resisted Posts, be sure to start looking at others' and think how to add your voice to share your thought leadership on topics of your expertise area. Note: if it is considered attorney advertisement in your jurisdiction's professional ethics, end the Post saying so.

Yes, it takes time to research, construct and compose a Post. You may want to consider being a thought leader by posting about once or twice a month. You must have some great things to say to your audiences, right?

If you are short on material worth posting, consider repurposing original material you published earlier elsewhere (on your blog or Facebook company page) and rewrite it as needed to appeal to a different professional audience on LinkedIn. Update your older material with pertinent, later details that arose. Add a story or observation about how this incident can be used effectively in the community or communities you serve.

Once posted, analyze the audience reactions (and there can be quite a few) with the analytics that LinkedIn provides for each Post. You can gain some insight into the industries and types of people reading your Posts.

Find the Analytics icon on your Activity page next to the number of views of the Post, and open it to let LinkedIn show you the generic details of who read the specific Post.

Marc W. Halpert posted this

Are you verifiably untrue on LinkedIn?
Marc W. Halpert on LinkedIn
January 27, 2017

44 **views** on this post

Is it the audience you sought to engage?

Yes? Keep posting. No? Tweak slowly and methodically in subsequent Posts so you achieve the resonance with the audience you seek. And remember, many people who you are *not* connected to on LinkedIn read your Posts by "following" you, and this will increase your impact. Be a wider thought leader.

Advice: keep your Post opinions professional. You have a fraction of a nanosecond to make an impression. If you use the wrong words, images, or nuances in your profile or Posts, it's on to the next competitor. Every word you write, every basic point you make, every decision to contact you lies in the balance: to consider or not consider you for the business. Like a trapeze act, one miss can end the performance.

The rhetoric of political discourse is certainly not proper in a LinkedIn Post, nor should we tolerate it. If it can be considered offensive to someone, leave it out.

Our power lies in the numbers of us who take the time and have the guts to criticize the offenders and suggest they concentrate otherwise. LinkedIn has overall community guidelines for published material we all agreed to when we joined.[6]

And if professional courtesy fails, LinkedIn has in its user agreement a standards-of-use policy we must adhere to,[7] as well as "dos and don'ts" for appropriate material and then also a published procedure for taking care of offensive material.[8]

For the vast majority of you, poor judgement on LinkedIn will never be an issue—just know policies are out there, and you have to adhere to them.

If you post quality and do so frequently, you will be admired and sought after. You never know who is reading your Post, how they will respond, how it can help them, and who they will send it to next. Your reach expands globally when you give your point of view in a professional forum. Be a spokesperson and thought leader. Nurture the personal learning network as you develop.

---

[6] https://www.linkedin.com/help/linkedin/answer/34593, Section 3.
[7] https://www.linkedin.com/legal/user-agreement, Section 8.2.
[8] https://www.linkedin.com/help/linkedin/answer/146.

Chapter 12

Experience as Marketing: Your Past Makes You Who You Are Today

This is a short chapter on a very important concept. Only you can tell what insights and wisdom your experience brings with you. I have a few pointers to help you as you perfect your narrative.

No matter how long ago you started to hone your business craft and skills, say, it was 1979, you must show how you developed throughout your career to who you are today and your "why" to create a vision ahead. In other words, your past dictates your present, and your present indicates your future career moves.

As discussed before in Chapter 4, and deliberately repeated here because these points are so important, this is not copy-paste from your résumé. The paper résumé is cast in ink and permanent (by definition, past-oriented), is expected to use bulleted factoids and metrics without context, is aimed at a

> "My LinkedIn page is visited far more regularly than the biography on my website. Maybe this is because everyone knows LinkedIn and how to search it, so it's quicker than looking for a website. Whatever the reason, in my experience LinkedIn seems to be the go-to source for information about me for my clients, colleagues, and even adversaries."
>
> **—Joseph Harris, Partner, White Harris PLLC, New York City, https://www.linkedin.com/in/ joseph-harrisesq**

different audience (a recruiter, human resources manager, or the ultimate employer) for a single purpose, to get a job, and then it's filed away.

Your LinkedIn profile is projected in whole sentences, with lots of room to explain to the reader, your professional community of colleagues and connections, why you bring certain attributes with you, and how you proceeded through your life's business. It is organic, in that it is changeable, can be referred to at all times, and is seen in its latest version online, both when, and especially when you're not, looking for a job.

In LinkedIn you must describe your past professional positions in terms of what you learned there or perfected in your career, and what you bring with you today. Then you should add comments on how you could use the present values in the future. A well-developed LinkedIn profile allows you to express WYDWYD *today,* based on the skills and character you have developed in your background *yesterday*, and aim for the rosy optimism of what the *future* will bring you and your firm or company.

Use search engine keywords here, too, like you did in the Summary and Headline. Make it read clearly yet cohesively, using terms that are recognizable to the human reader as well as to the electronic keyword search engine.

Open a narrative tied to each job in your career, giving yourself more commentary space for positions you spent more time at versus shorter-term jobs. Keep the voice, tone, style, and format the same throughout as you write reflections on each position you held. Add rich graphics, video, PDFs, slide decks (be sure you have the owner's approval) to the job position to further demonstrate what you achieved there and complement what you experienced. Use "I" and power verbs, not the third person with weak verbs like "make" and "do".

Slow down for a few minutes, or as long as it takes, and re-read your Experience section out loud: does it tell us *why you do what you do* and *how you want others to know you do it?* Or are you still resisting telling your full story? Probably your draft will need some tweaking, so continually edit the Experience section to reinforce in different words what you already said in the Headline and the Intro.

You'd better be complete, before someone interprets whatever you left out, for you. Their assumptions will never be good ones. Tell us fully and openly, in your own words, what each job in your Experience meant to your trajectory. Yes, you should write your own history, with more contextual facts and more color. Just be sure you are adding more meat to the LinkedIn profile Experience from your résumé's skeletal bones.

LinkedIn recognizes that not everyone has a linear career path. Sometimes it makes perfect sense for large gaps in experience to occur. Is your career a patchwork of great experience and achievement? Have you held multi-industry, different roles without an immediately obvious "classical" progression? Are you embarking on an encore career? Are you a "recovering" lawyer, or a new professional practitioner after a career spent in another industry? Provide some guidance to the reader to explain your out-of-the-ordinary, yet very valid reasons for your career path and still tell your unique story:

- Emphasize the new skills, activities, and accolades from that earlier period, being confident and upbeat.
- "At-Home Parent" is a valid Experience entry with its own narrative of what it meant and what you learned.
- Show the part-time positons(s) you held in that period that helped you develop new skills and stay current with technology.
- You can accumulate several short positions into a larger functional one with an overarching description.
- If a part-time position became a full-time position, tell us. It reflects well on you.

Just stay clear, concise, and confident in bridging the different aspects of your past, present, and future while expressing WYDWYD.

Naming the companies you worked for is one thing, but try to get their logos to appear by clicking "change company" from the edit screen and start typing the company name. Select the company name when it appears and so does its logo. Logos are highly recognizable and memorable to the casual reader at a glance. For many companies, though they may now be gone, the logos endure and are noticed in a visual scan of your Experience history.

In each position you held, tell that personal development story using past, present, future, and *how* and *why*—far superior to a résumé listing who and what.

Chapter 13

Using Multimedia on Intro and Experience Sections

If a picture is worth a thousand words, rich multimedia material on LinkedIn can be worth a million. As mentioned before, LinkedIn makes it very easy to provide a graphic expression of you and your work in either of two places: (1) in your Intro and (2) within your Experience; here you can select where to place it, job by job.

So first here's a little tech talk. And I will deviate from my promise to not approach this step-by-step. It's just that multimedia is all too often absent on professionals' LinkedIn profiles, since they assume it is hard to upload—not so, and hence my desire to escort you through the process.

LinkedIn accepts graphics on your profile in any of the numerous formats listed on http://embed.ly/providers, so let's just say you'll be able to attach almost anything you want to add to accentuate your work. I have worked on using graphics for myself and for clients, and the most common formats certainly work perfectly fine: video, PDF, slide decks, audio files, podcasts, photos, among other graphics. You just need to be certain you own the rights to the graphic or have the approval (written is best) from the owner.

Intro Section

Note the place that you can add supplemental graphics to enhance your Intro section (the narrative beneath your headshot and Headline), either uploaded to LinkedIn from your hard drive or with a link from elsewhere. Be sure these graphics pertain to you at a high level, rather than tied to a certain career position. You want to give an overall impression of *why* you, consistent with your Intro's general point of view.

Experience Section

A graphic is similarly presented in the Experience, meant here to complement a particular job you hold now or held in the past. You can see a series of icons to choose from to add a graphic.

That part of the process is mechanical, yet the overall effect is that a graphic further illustrates a point or concept you are making in your Intro or an aspect of your job in your Experience. What's important to realize (and to repeat this earlier point) is that the graphic in the Intro must be generic enough to highlight your entire experience, and the graphic tied to a job in your Experience must be just that: demonstrating pictorially an aspect of your work at that job at that time. Choose wisely.

As you add more graphics, you will see them line up in a row three-across, then the reader clicks an arrow to see the next three, etc.

A description, color thumbnail, good quality audio and/or video, and mentioning the duration of the media are all clues for the reader to choose to view your material—make the description pique their interest. The point is that different things will stimulate the reader enough to open your graphic. You just have to provide the detail and a call to action to see more about you. Your message has to flow, generally repeated a couple of times in different terms in each section of your profile, such that it conveys a consistent message: WYDWYD. It also demonstrates your comfort level in showing your value in different media for different purposes and to certain audiences.

And at the risk of repeating an earlier point, today it's common, even expected, to use video to prove your point, as the most immediate and memorable medium—good quality video, that is. Certainly the other media are still valid, alone or in combination. You can craft a valuable slide deck, speak eloquently in a podcast, publish a purposeful whitepaper in PDF format, sure, but can you speak well in as many media as your audience expects you to, especially before a video camera (or increasingly, a smartphone) and make great points quickly to achieve your messaging? Perhaps your video persona and message will put you over the top to be hired ahead of the competitor.

And you can be sure that people recall best what they see and hear simultaneously, and that should be you, via your well-crafted message and your high-quality video. But memories are still short. So pick your medium and add video to your repertoire as a visual complement to what your LinkedIn profile says in words. And use it well and frequently (repurpose it!) in different touchpoints with your readership.

Chapter 14

Showcasing Your Publications: Show Us What You Write, All Right?

Have you just published something in an online professional journal, an e-zine, or a newspaper; guest blogged; or written a chapter or authored an entire book? Or were you quoted in a publication? Did you appear in someone else's video or audio broadcast?

Memorialize it to LinkedIn in the Publications subsection of your profile. Different from a shared update, which disappears from the LinkedIn updates page in a few days, the Publications subsection remains a permanent part of your personal profile, *only if you* add it.

Once published, online or on paper, you should let the right subset of your LinkedIn world know:

- Contribute the news you were published in a LinkedIn shared update to your connections on the day of publication.
- Next, memorialize it in the Publications subsection of your LinkedIn personal profile.
- Speak about and share the link with a brief comment on your relevant Group pages.
- If allowed by your original publisher and appropriate, repurpose the material to a Post.

- Compose a new Post along the lines of "What I learned from the reaction to my recent article in {XYZ}."

But tell us on LinkedIn! Share good news so we can root you on, because we want to help, and we reciprocate the publicity. Yes, that's why it's called *social* media.

Consider placing the body of written professional work you have produced in your career as your personal library of materials in your Publications subsection. First, be sure you know where you have it squirreled away—a hard drive, the cloud, a website on which it originally appeared.

Keep in mind that it's perfectly fine to curate your own material—select carefully. You do not want to show everything you ever wrote. Use discretion. Don't list work that is too old (this century only please), and certainly don't list anything that is off topic from your existing skill set that makes the reader wonder what you really do for a living.

But despite what I just said about the age of the material, what is more important is the perceived professional or academic quality of the piece. Some writing you produced may have been sent to discrete populations and audiences, so use your judgement: a high-quality piece is nonetheless worth attaching to your Publication section on LinkedIn, showing your ability to write well, a lost skill in today's workforce, and a differentiator.

Writing samples are very important aspects of getting an assignment. If the ones you chose can demonstrate an ability to convey complex legal/financial/technical ideas in a concise digestible way for the lay community, you can also effectively show it on LinkedIn with a proper foreword to the reader about why you chose to showcase this and the factual backdrop for context.

As you add your written pieces to the Publication section of your personal LinkedIn profile, here is what you might see as a (completed) entry, ready to save to LinkedIn.

Obviously you need access to the title, publication name, and date it appeared. Be sure it is available online, as you will need the URL for the document.

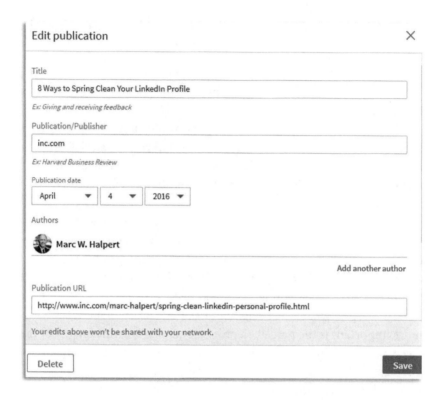

If you have it on your hard drive, upload it to your cloud storage and backup subscription (Dropbox, Box, Google Drive, etc.) and insert its URL.

Be sure you give credit to any co-authors, guest writers, interviewers, journalists, etc., and refer to their LinkedIn profiles in the author field so it shows on their profile as well (get their OK to do so). Finally, add a short (and I mean short) description that gives the reader an idea of what they are about to see when they open the link to your written piece. Make this a marketing opportunity to get them to *want* to open it and share it. Answer: how will this help someone? What's in it for the reader (and hopefully those he or she decides to share it with)?

And be creative as to what types of material you add to your Publications. Quotes in books and articles, radio spots, and TV interviews do not fit anywhere else in your LinkedIn profile, so the Publication section is the place for these types of hybrid publications and broadcasts. Media is blurring the old lines between written, visual, and verbal these days.

Add all your past publications, one by one. But as you do so, you will see that LinkedIn added that newest article you uploaded way at the bottom of the Publications subsection by default. (I always mentally ask myself after I add a new publication, why would LinkedIn deliberately show my most recent publication *last*?) Perhaps by the time you read this, LinkedIn has fixed this.

There *is* a fix and it's pretty easy. You just have to know where to look. Click "Edit Profile" and move down to your Publication subsection. Anything there that you mouse over highlights in another color, probably gray.

And off to the right corner of each publication, you will see a double-headed arrow (outlined in a box above for emphasis). Hold your left mouse button down over the double-headed arrow. Now you can drag that entire article up to the top, and as you do this to your other publications, you can stack-rank them chronologically now with the most recent at the top. Or alphabetically if you choose, or organize them by publisher—these latter two options are unusual but can be done.

Do this for all past articles, and remember when you add the next article you publish to drag the most recent one you list to the top. Make your latest and/or greatest publication topmost and noticeable.

Chapter 15

Volunteer: Do Good

You and your firm are well represented when you serve on a board(s) at a nonprofit, volunteer, or donate your time, money, and expertise to help an organization(s) work more effectively in its mission.

LinkedIn allows you to *mention* the selfless difference you make in your community by adding your nonprofit position(s), ranging from an ad hoc volunteer to a board seat and/or officer position in the Volunteer section of your personal profile. Please note I suggest "mention," and let the reader draw his or her own conclusions based on how richly you word your work efforts at the nonprofit organization you serve.

My point is to suggest you add some qualitative narrative to your volunteer position(s) by describing what professional expertise and time you contribute, which, when said well, will further show your community dedication. This is not a place to be overly modest or conversely, advertise. Your commitment and service are humbly donated and demonstrated on your profile, but you can show us how you make a difference there.

Another tendency I see is to list a board presidency as a job in your Experience section. I think this fits far better in the Volunteer section instead. It will not break up the reader's following your career trajectory with a nonprofit position distraction in between the professional career movements you engineered.

Are you looking to become active as a volunteer, as an expert offering pro bono assistance or offering your specific knowledge for a board position but don't know where to find the open opportunities? LinkedIn for Good, a division dedicated to volunteer and veteran issues, operates a global "job board" of sorts where you can match yourself to an opening in your area. To learn more, go to https://volunteer.linkedin.com. From this link, you can peruse openings in a database and begin to read about the organizations showing the openings from their LinkedIn "company" profile pages (yes, nonprofits need to have a LinkedIn company profile page; more on that in Chapter 27 for all types of firms, yours included).

Jump in by offering your expertise by visiting volunteer.linkedin. com.

When you select any of the buttons on that Web page, you see pages of opportunities to select for your interest, location, etc. and level of commitment to learn even more about an open volunteer position.

Congratulations on your willingness to help others. You, and thus your firm, will look better outwardly to your community, and you will feel better inwardly as a result of your selfless assistance to others in need. Opportunities for good deeds abound on LinkedIn.

Chapter 16

Organizations You Belong to Can Add Breadth to Your Profile

The amazing thing about organizations we choose to join is that they accurately reflect our interests, our passions, our field of work, and our quality commitment, and this is where we can meet others with similar leanings and pursue business with the best of the best.

You likely already align yourself with some or several. Start filling in the Organizations section, telling LinkedIn readers of your alliances in one or more organization(s) that is/are *especially* prominent in your business professional world. LinkedIn allows you to give each its/their own line listing and write a short explanation of its/their meaning to you.

Write in prose what groups you participate in and explain your involvement. You have lots of room.

Note that if your membership in this group transcends occupation positions held during your membership, you can ignore choosing a specific occupation from the drop-down box.

Note that if you're a multi-preneur, that tip will help you, as it does me. And, this section makes it very easy for dual designation holders to shine with varied academic and professional designations.

Avoid acronyms when listing the rest of your organizations; be aware that familiarity with industry-specific initials and acronyms may not be universal. One group I belong to is abbreviated "ICE," and I am

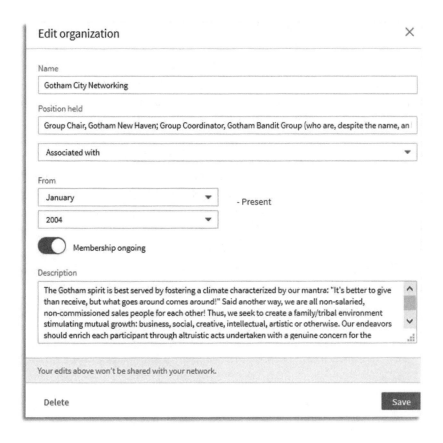

certain that the three-letter acronym doesn't tell you very much, so I chose to type out its full name: Intellectual Capital Exchange. As its full name suggests, it is a high-functioning, more cerebral business referral group than most.

Of course, if you hold an officer position in the organization, let us know what you do there. That's important to describe yet often left out by accident.

For the rest of the myriad clubs, professional groups, bar associations, membership groups, and networking organizations you participate in, listing them is fine. When you list them under Additional Organizations, separate them by commas so the casual reader can peruse it (and thus know more about you) better.

Keep your list current. Add new organizations you join. Delete those you phase out from; be mindful that organizations merge or die away, so they need to be renamed or deleted from this section, too.

Ensure the list shows your full range of professional interests, activity, and contribution level, as your perception as a businessperson with one or more professional interests may be essential to differentiating you from the competition.

Not all organizations are business oriented. Show all sides of your personality. One caveat: if you are concerned that a group you belong to belies a political, special interest, or religious affiliation that can shadow the objectivity of a decision maker about you or encourage an uninformed assumption, only you can decide to include it, or leave it out, or handle this in a narrative about your involvement, and *why*, in the group.

Showing your involvement professionally (and otherwise) in groups is an expected and informative eye into your personality, as well.

Chapter 17

Certifications: Show Them to Differentiate You

You worked long and hard to attain the professional designation(s) and certifications that you need to dominate in your expertise area. Or perhaps you sought them even if not required but for the self-satisfaction of being the best in your field. And as you renew them, you take CLEs, other classwork, and/or retest to stay on top of the field. You earned them, you know your clients and prospects evaluate whether or not you have the right credentials, and you should proudly show them on your LinkedIn profile. Congratulations on any and all—required, optional, or both.

These designations distinguish you from the competition, as they should. To those prospects shopping for the best expert with the right credentials, please do not be hesitant to tell what they mean: to you, to your industry, and most importantly, to the client's success.

Does the casual reader know what these designations even mean, as they are normally expressed as an acronym after your name? Don't confuse them; perhaps you need to cut back to the most important designations if you have quite a few.

But do list them in the Certifications section of your LinkedIn personal profile, explain which professional organization awards them (again, no initials, spell out the name of the association, describe those not commonly known, and add the URL of the organization's home page), what year you received the certification, and revise the listing as necessary to show that you keep them up-to-date. These details are vital, showing your attention to detail within your field. Don't let a reader make an incorrect assumption based on something you left out.

Any designation or certification that eventually expires must be shown as kept current: list its beginning date to present. If it expired, don't show the credential. Yes, it may no longer pertain to you, but any negative assumption about letting a certification lapse is too hard to explain adequately. If there is a license or certification number associated with the designation, please show it on your profile; failure to do so may affect your perception negatively, as if you are hiding something. Yes, that's how some people think.

You have a fair amount of room to describe each certification, and be sure to do that well. Think about what is needed to be known about each certification that will help give a reader unfamiliar with your field the confidence that you are the right person for the opportunity they may have in mind. Perhaps the reader is from another industry and needs a bit of explanation.

For dual-designation folks, this is a great place to show how one certification complements the others you have earned, to accentuate your overall excellence and achievement, much like adjectives to add to the quality of your work. Anytime a client recommends you on LinkedIn, you can have them add language about how your two (or more) designations made a real difference in the work that was needed. More on Recommendation strategies comes later in Chapter 24 and Chapter 37 (guest Carol Greenwald's chapter on ethical considerations).

Stand out proudly. In some industries, you are required to show you passed certain certification hurdles, such as wealth advisory, banking, financial analysis, public accounting, and health care management. Notches like this in the stick are worth accentuating for the role they play in your analytical capabilities. There is no better place to do this than in your LinkedIn profile.

Chapter 18

Honors and Awards: Don't Be Shy

Much like the chapter before, it's also important to show honors and awards you have received (you have earned!) from professional organizations, associations, business groups, and the nonprofits you support, thanking you for your service above and beyond, differentiating you from competitors—all especially rewarding when peers honor you.

Recognition by others for your job well done is worth portraying on your LinkedIn profile because we want to surround ourselves, and when needed, hire those who are better than the rest. That indicates to us that their work will shine beyond the norm and will provide service that excels. That makes the project a success and presages that the research and implemented changes are worth the time and effort and money.

And like the Certifications, be certain to advise us what the award was recognizing: from your past work, who gave it. In other words, give us context as to why this is meaningful, to you, and thus to us:

"I was chosen from among 250 applicants . . ."
"My work in streamlining and saving costs and workload was recognized for my changing from . . . to . . ."

Describe the honor in terms of the skills that you already possessed and what you contributed—the unique circumstances that brought about this special recognition. This is not a laundry list of metrics, but rather a high-level overview of you being the best person at the right time to ideally address the circumstances and be recognized for it.

And remember to describe if it is an annual award and if your "reign" as awardee has passed. There's no harm in it drifting into the history books. Remarkable honorees are recalled fondly and memorably.

Chapter 19

Skills and Endorsements: Making Sweet Lemonade

I always call the Skills section on LinkedIn "the section I love to hate." In my estimation, it's valuable when used properly, but it has been so overused—no, I will call it misused.

Settle back, this section is long and important; it's here to help you with this one single somewhat troublesome section and prevent you from getting into ethical and factual hot water.

LinkedIn places weight on Skills and Endorsements in the search function. These skills are becoming searchable terms. That in itself means you have to pay careful attention to this chapter. The area allocated to skills in your profile is worth some marketing ideas to make it work well for you. For me personally, because I follow the rules I am about to instruct you on, it now works well enough that my original misgivings are softening. Used effectively and intelligently, it can tell a lot in a few words, quickly. And that's valuable, so let's make it actually mean more to help you.

Start by asking your firm's web designer what SEO keywords are worked into your company website, to bring up words and phrases someone would use to find you in a search (either on Google in the case of the work by the web designer or on LinkedIn for your purposes in this book), then write these search terms into a list. Second, make a list of the SEO keywords you wrote into your revised Headline, Intro, and Experience section narratives.

k of the words in those sections that describe your skills.
and amending the words, culling out nonskills and mas-
ısed words in both lists (there may be duplication) until
you have about fifteen or twenty of them; complementary overlap is OK
among them, as they indicate variations on a skill. Look at competitors'
skills if you can actually see them. Look at colleagues' and coworkers'
and vendors' LinkedIn Skills sections. Did they list some skills you had
missed? Whittle the resulting list down to the best twenty or so that you
can come up with.

Then run tests using these keywords in the Search to see if you
and some competitors and colleagues come up in the search results.
If you don't come up, continue refining and keeping notes. When you
are satisfied with the list of skills, enter these search keywords into
your Skills section, and as you begin typing them in, LinkedIn might
just suggest others in contexts you have not thought of. Keep that
list going.

Note that "management" is not a skill. "Finance" is not one either.
They are textbooks on a bookshelf. Find the right set of words and
phrases to describe your skills, even if LinkedIn seems to lead you to use
diluted skill terms. Rise above that. Refine these skill labels in ways that
reflect the honest and beneficial skills you bring to the proverbial table,
such as "law firm operations management" or "financial risk assess-
ment." You are more likely to stand out in a search for these terms if you
list them in your Skills.

As we said earlier, LinkedIn is a gigantic granular searchable database of respectable business pros seeking others. Its search function pri-
marily queries four profile sections: Headline, Intro, Experience, and
Skills. Remember, later you can always go back to these sections and
knit in more descriptive and usable keywords that come out of your
skills since you know you need to make regular revisions; cohesively,
they feed each other.

Once listed, be aware that you can reorder the skills you list by
simply dragging and dropping them with your mouse. This way you
can accentuate the skills you want the casual reader to see, and react
to, first.

Endorsements by people who do not have direct experience with your skill, despite the fact they endorsed you with good intention or out of carelessness, need to be edited out. Again no worries, losing their endorsement is not an issue because they can neither help describe your skills anyhow nor assist you in being in the search results. Besides, LinkedIn does not notify them that you deleted their endorsement.

This section was redesigned in February 2017 to reduce the number of tiny thumbnail photos of your endorsers and thus accentuate your skill set more clearly. The result is a much better Skills section.

Now let's look at ways to preempt endorsements from those who do not really know your skills. Again some unavoidable how-to steps follow in this chapter, as it is vitally important to maintain good profile control and effectively market your brand. Start by clicking the "Adjust

Endorsement Settings" at the bottom left of the Skills and Endorsements section, and you will see the following:

Endorsements		✕
Manage how you receive and give endorsements		
I want to be endorsed	Yes	⬤▬
Include me in endorsement suggestions to my connections	No	▬◯
Show me suggestions to endorse my connections	No	▬◯

I agree you want to be endorsed but suggest you opt out of allowing LinkedIn to recommend you for endorsements to others, and decline allowing LinkedIn to suggest who you should endorse. Be sure the first rocker switch is at "yes" and the other two are "no." You and your connections need to make independent decisions on who to endorse.

Recall how we said earlier that you control everything that is in your profile from third parties. This is one such great example, and you must stay on top of each email from LinkedIn telling you when someone has endorsed you so you can check the integrity of that endorsement and keep the data and facts straight from your point of view.

I appreciate LinkedIn's default setting of sending you an email every time someone endorses you so you can keep it or delete it to comply with ethical considerations and reality. To repeat something stated earlier, every notification on LinkedIn appears in your LinkedIn messages and is copied to the email address you have on file with LinkedIn. That means two notifications of each endorsement come to you, so you really should be able to know about them as they occur, one way or another, and delete endorsements as needed.

Suppose I wanted to review (and remove if needed) incorrect endorsers for my skill in Training; I click that skill by name, and I can review a box of all my endorsers for that particular skill.

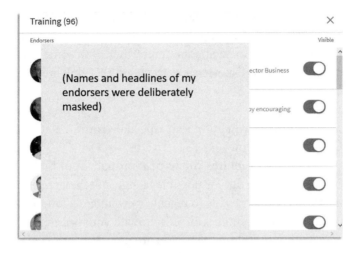

Training (96) ✕

Endorsers Visible

(Names and headlines of my endorsers were deliberately masked)

ector Business

oy encouraging

If an endorser whose thumbnail photo and name appears to the right in the list has never attended one of my training sessions, I believe it honest and advisable to move the rocker switch to the left next to his or her name and then click "save" so he or she no longer appears as an endorser of my Training skill. Again, that person will not receive any notification from LinkedIn.

Yes, it takes effort to cull out endorsers who are not appropriate. But it is a worthwhile investment that may take some bulk time initially but will be far less time consuming as you keep up with this maintenance chore.

Why is this important? For attorneys, be sure to remove any endorsements that are not factual, as this can be perceived as a failure to keep up with them and may contravene ethics rules under your bar association guidelines. More on Skills and Endorsements come later in Chapter 37 (guest Carol Greenwald's chapter on ethical considerations). Why else?

Suppose I need a referral of a trusted financial advisor for baby boomers with older parents. You are one of those financial advisors, and I may know you from a brief meeting at a chamber event. Another day I am meeting with Carolyn, who has already endorsed you for your skills in Eldercare Financial Planning, and I explain why I need her input on the short list of quality candidates. Ahead of my conversation I did my homework and see you and she are mutual LinkedIn connections.

I delved further in your profile and I saw she endorsed you for a skill in Eldercare Financial Planning. I ask her during my meeting how she knows your skill in that area. She stammers, then with some embarrassment admits she has no experience with you in that skill area.

How do you look?

How does she feel?

What do I think of you both now, especially you?

Have I wasted my time?

Uh oh, your work requires you to be thorough. Your brand is to be reliable and have an eye out for possible technical (tax, legal, documentary) roadblocks and to be able to react to new financial opportunities.

But your LinkedIn profile is out of sync with your brand. You missed something. I think to myself that if you are not very complete, missing details in your own profile, how will you handle my financial details in a complex financial situation? Will you skip over something that might cause problems down the road?

Is this farfetched? No, not really. I hear real stories like this frequently, and it's uncomfortable for all involved. No one wants to feel embarrassed. Worse, you allowed an endorsement from someone with no real experience with your skill in that area, and your pristine reputation is now spotty in my view. Your mistake or not, I may no longer consider you and move along to someone else. It is best not to allow yourself to be placed in such a situation, especially because it's quick and easy to fix an errant endorsement before it gets noticed. Negative perceptions can be long term.

Once you have settled on the right skills to portray, it's time to edit out the old ones. Whenever you delete a skill, all the connections who recognized you for that old skill no longer appear as endorsers for that skill. That's not a problem—the skill term you just deleted was deficient anyway. You'll replace it with a better one, right? Besides, it's not the quantity of endorsers, it's the quality of the skills you show and are searchable for.

You can delete skills completely by clicking the blue pencil at the top of the Skills section then "x" at the left side of the skill cartouche. Zoom, it's gone (and the endorsers that go along with that skill, but no worries).

Finally, you can change the order now—to match the order of importance you believe these skills are to the business(es) you operate. You can click, drag, and drop the skill to the position you want it to be seen. The order of the skills appears by the number of endorsements, and your top most endorsed skills will appear on your personal profile with the thumbnail photos of the endorsers. The next most endorsed skills you have will appear as cartouches (no thumbnail photos) below that.

If I were an attorney and I wanted to query and add skills that started with the word "legal," LinkedIn is generous in offering skill names that others may have used.

Please do not be limited to what they list. Think outside the suggestion box. Be true to what key skill words you believe you will be searched for yet are confident that you possess that skill.

Alternatively, if "Legal Compliance for Commercial Insurance" is a better skill descriptor than "Legal Compliance" (and it is, if that pertains to you directly), overwrite the suggested skill and add it in the box. Feel free to augment an existing one or compose your own skill.

You can list up to fifty skills. That's a lot, and perhaps too many for you, yet multi-preneurs may need that many to cover all their generic and specific skills in multiple industries. Some may overlap; others may be specific to one or more of your concurrent industries.

What's the upshot? I used to hate the Skills section, and now I really find it useful when monitored—lemonade from lemons. Choose your skills carefully so others will endorse you for skills they know you possess, and the most pertinent skills appear toward the top of your listing. If you need to rework your Skills, do so (be creative yet realistic). Once you have made a number of changes, it's OK to let your connections know that you have made changes via a status update.

Rewrite and tweak, tailor, and cull out the folks who thought endorsing you for all your skills is a compliment. It wasn't after all. It takes work. Stay on top of it. Your reputation is at stake.

Chapter 20

Courses Taken/Teaching: Continuing Education Is a Two-Way Street

We have to stay on top of the latest trends and advance our knowledge to benefit our clients. Most professional practices require completion of CLEs and other classwork, either mandated by the government, industry, an association, or provided by the firm itself or delivered via an educational institution. Courses are provided in person, or online, or in a hybrid method such as in a live broadcast course.

Universities see a goldmine in onsite or online courses aimed at experienced professionals and sharp new managers.

Sometimes the course topic may not seem to match the industry we work in (certificate in managerial accounting for an insurance pro, for example) or may be general education to advance our business savvy (a negotiation strategy course for an architect). Perhaps your brokerage company sent you to a mini-MBA course.

In whatever format you take the course, and whatever the topic, if it is worthy of your going through it, and beneficial to your clientele, it should be important enough to list on your LinkedIn profile in the Courses section.

Keep these listed chronologically and with a brief description of the provider of the course, the date(s), and the credential you received for the training, if applicable. Briefly tell the reader why the course was needed and the benefit you received that will help future clients.

Conversely, if you teach a course, tell us in the Courses section, but twist it a bit as I did for courses I have taught. You lead off with the company name you worked in at the time, and fill in the course name and number, course description, semester taught, and URL if available.

---

2   **Courses**   🖉

Teaching "LinkedIn: A Job Seeker's Best Friend" for Larchmont-Mamaroneck Center for Continuing Education May and October 2016 https://www.lmcce.org/pro

Co-taught at Norwalk Community College "The Essential Nonprofit: Creating & Operating a Nonprofit Organization" Spring 2012 2 sections

---

Here, I am using the scarce space in the Courses section of my LinkedIn profile to show I am educating and assisting my colleagues in my area of expertise rather than taking a course.

If you ever taught a course, you know how much work goes into it and how rewarding it is to explain to colleagues why you are passionate about your field of work. You deserve to recognize yourself for it.

Make each course you took, or taught, reflect well on you, using the right words and reasons to make you stand away and apart from the competitors.

Chapter 21

Formal Education as a Prerequisite; Alumni Search Function

This section is aimed at all professional practitioners, and it will be brief.

Show all your education: college, grad school, and the years attended. Period.

I even show my high school and years.

Are you reluctant to have someone calculate your age from your graduation year? My reply is: can they see your headshot? Can they see your first job out of school? Then they have an idea how old you are. They should be hiring your experience, skill set, and sage advice. That comes with time spent in your field. Get over your age being mentally tabulated. Stop fearing others knowing how old you really are, the prime reason people leave this statistic out. You have to do this. There, I said it.

There is a very valuable advantage of showing your graduation year: your fellow alums can search for you on LinkedIn; you can search for them. Click the name of your school under Education on your profile. The resulting page has a button marked See Alumni at the top left.

In this case, because LinkedIn knows I already placed the University of Virginia (UVA) on my profile, I am directed to this mini search tool to find fellow alums, by name.

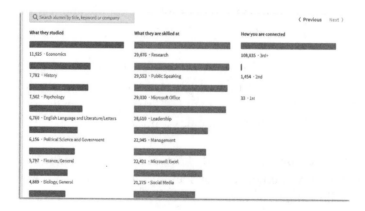

Or I can search the UVA set if I had a subject to query: by using any search term for this university's subset of the LinkedIn population, mentioning our mutual alma mater in an inquiry to a fellow alum allows a warmer introduction, and thus a better chance at a good connection even if we attended in different decades, better than my baldly approaching the target as a complete stranger.

I have reconnected to old friends by manipulating the "attended" years and found classmates, well on their way in their own careers. They can find you, too. That's why your graduation year is important to place on your LinkedIn profile.

The analytics on each graduating class can be quite revealing. The first three bar charts (where they live, where they work, what they do) appear above, and if you click the "Next" in the far right margin, you get three more.

See, listing your skills on your profile is again important, and they are correlated here, too. And if you click "Show More" at the bottom of either of these two sets, you get even more detail for each analytic.

Finally, below these six analytic bar charts are thumbnails of fellow alums (set the years you attended at the top right) to review and ask to connect to. Mine is as shown.

Marc W. Halpert
LinkedIn coach & group trainer
helping you look amazing-er...

Next to your thumbnail are other fellow alums you may already know or used to know. Each person's name is clickable to take you to his or her personal profile page. You can see the person's Headline and geographic location as well.

How do you use this? Let your professional curiosity and imagination roam. You may reconnect with an old study group mate, a fellow alum who is now chief executive officer (CEO) in a firm who could consider you on the short list of advisory service providers, a colleague in a firm across the country should you ever need his or her opinion, who knows? This little tool provides a new, additionally more granular search for you to benefit from. It's just not widely known enough, until now.

Sharing a common university experience is always a great way to surround yourself with others who recall the "good old days" and re-find old friends on an alumni site to do that with. LinkedIn has just that. You can search for all graduates from your college or grad school days and reacquaint. These old friends are more apt to tip business your way, because you both share the common educational experience. It's human nature for likes to prefer likes.

Chapter 22

Nonwork Interests: All Work and No Play Is Dull

It's certainly acceptable, in fact, advisable, to talk about your outside interests and passions, hobbies, favorite teams, foods you crave, and travel you embark on. You have a life outside the office, right?

Then tell us what else makes you fascinating. It's part of your brand. It's a segment of your personality that you enrich and makes us remember you, because we might further click with you, want to engage with you. Emotionally and intellectually buying into your brand, as I quoted Lois Geller in Chapter 1, right?

In the March 2017 desktop user interface change, the Additional Information section was eliminated. However, consider augmenting your Intro to include personal comments about your outside interests to give you profile depth and reflect on who you really are, in work and in your home life.

It's a human reaction for us to be attracted to people with similar interests. We are predisposed to buy or consider buying your services, when we connect on some emotional level. We buy with more than our intellect.

Most of all, it makes you memorable when you offer a little bit more than just the professional self, but another part of you that we can relate to. Here's a true story: at a recent party a friend approached me and asked, "You know a lot of attorneys. I have a colleague who needs a great divorce attorney, do you know anyone?" As I flipped through my mental

Rolodex, I preselected a few. Before I would refer anyone in particular, I asked, "Tell me a bit about the client—what are some of the personality aspects that will make her work well with an attorney I refer?"

After all, this is a deeply personal matter. The response contained a personality trait, interest, or attribute that the friend's colleague has, one that would mesh well with the best of the fits on my short list of one or two divorce attorneys I referred. Again, it's important to be memorable for a number of different elements beyond work and professional skills. Personality plays an important role.

And please, an admonition: it's not necessary to show birthdates— in my humble opinion, no one cares, even though LinkedIn gives you a place to mention them.

The same comment goes with your marital status. The only exception I recall was the same divorce attorney mentioned just above whom I coached and who proudly mentions on her profile she was once married, now divorced, so it is clear she knows the process from the inside out and is a better counselor to her clients as a result. Now that's properly marketing her marital status to help her clients.

It should be noted in this chapter that mentioning religious and political affiliations is a personal decision. Be sure you use factual statements that cannot be construed as overtly controversial; the latter should be avoided. Be personal but be professional!

And finally one more piece of advice: carefully choose the interests you show. Beware that some people make rash and unwarranted decisions based on very little information and could exclude you from consideration for a project or potential business opportunity. Just because you have an interest, possibly perceived by some as extreme, you do not *have to* list it. Use discretion and intelligence, as I know you will. If in doubt, leave it out. I am sure you have other things to show us: focus on the other less contentious aspects of your persona beyond your work.

Chapter 23

Call on Me, or Contact Me, OK?

The phone rings once in a while. Not like the old days when it was the primary means of communication. Perhaps in your industry, or your firm, the phone is still as important, as it once was to me, but think of the emails, texts, tweets, and so on, that have supplanted faxes and oral conversation in business.

There are so many ways to communicate. Everyone has a preferred method. Embrace them all. Some methods aggregate around age brackets, industries, educational levels, nationalities, and so on. Learn the best practices in using them all.

Make yourself approachable in every method by succinctly naming and listing all of them on your LinkedIn profile: email address, phone number, Twitter handle, Facebook name, blog name, website, and so on, in your Contact and Personal Info section on the rightmost column of your profile.

Note that these are only visible to your LinkedIn connections (a privilege of your connection), again a reason to carefully choose your connections ahead of time and reserving that private information to those you vetted and trust.

One additional note is that you can further control what appears on your public page by going to Edit Your Public Profile, a wide-ranging privacy setting,[9] and clicking or unclicking the selections in the rightmost

---

[9] https://www.linkedin.com/public-profile/settings?trk=nprofile-public-profile-settings-redirect.

column. I keep them all open; you may differ with me and can control this yourself.

However you manage this, do not make getting a hold of you difficult, even if you are not connected to the other person on LinkedIn. It may preclude contact that could become business.

You can see from the top line of my contact details that my LinkedIn URL is linkedin.com/in/marchalpert; it's secure and mine forever.

In fact, each of us receives one when we start a LinkedIn membership. Yours may still end with letters and numbers. But I have gone one step further and personalized mine at the end with my name. You should do that too by going to the same privacy setting link as above,[10] and at the top right, customize by keying your name into the white box at the end of your public profile URL—no extraneous letters or numbers, just your name if you can.

> "My most recent client was looking for someone to do a presentation on women entrepreneurs and philanthropy. She found articles I had written on the topic but not my contact info. She found me using LinkedIn Inmail."
>
> —Geri Stengel, President and Founder, Ventureneer, New York City, https://www.linkedin.com/in/geristenge

---

[10] https://www.linkedin.com/public-profile/settings?trk=nprofile-public-profile-settings-redirect.

If your name is already claimed, add *Esq.* or *CPA* or a number at the end to claim it for yourself. You may have to get creative. Once it's saved, it's yours, and you can use it everywhere:

- Business card
- Email signature
- Letterhead
- Marketing materials
- Slide decks and handouts
- CV

Use your LinkedIn URL as a contact placeholder in your marketing communications so anyone can find you and read about you as you self-brand in your very best ways.

Before a meeting, review attendees' LinkedIn profiles for clues about how to make yourself more interactive, bringing down the unease that is so prevalent in any new meeting between strangers. Start with a question or two about how the target knows your common friend(s). When did you last see or work with that colleague? It is amazing how fast the ice melts with small talk at the beginning, well beyond the weather or other tired topics.

Use your smartphone LinkedIn app to refresh your memory just before you step into a meeting. That has served me well in spare moments while waiting.

Research the speaker's LinkedIn profile ahead of a presentation. You may be able to ask a more in-depth question and gain important insights from that expert.

When both parties interact in a more personalized way, it makes for a more efficient and more effective outcome.

Memorize the target's headshot just in case you have an unplanned meeting ahead of time. An impromptu greeting to that person might just impress him or her, even before you formally meet.

It's all about familiarity and comfort. You have a powerful tool, so using it is just a matter of practice and prior planning to reach out and/or be memorable.

But sometimes it's hard to get access to the target or you just don't know how to make contact to get the target's attention. This brings us to LinkedIn's Inmail, a communication tool that one person can use to reach out to another via LinkedIn, especially useful when he or she is not connected. Recall that once you agree to connect, you can freely message each other on LinkedIn, and each message is copied to your email box. Inmail is different: it is allocated in limited supply, and the number you have is based on the LinkedIn Premium subscription plan, (or not) that you have.

Because they are rare, they normally command attention from the recipient; however, they are even more powerful when used effectively as well. LinkedIn offers its own recommendations to make Inmails more responsive.[11]

The following are a few of my tips:

- Use Inmail if you want to avoid the gatekeeper at the phone and proceed right to the executive you want to communicate with.

> "One client that I work with has multiple departments . . . one of my contacts there, who I had worked with occasionally, had left the organization and I was not aware until she made a post on LinkedIn noting the change in career. I immediately sent out a note of congrats and told her that I looked forward to staying in touch with her. About four months later, I received an Inmail from this connection requesting some information and quotes on a project at her new place of business. She had told me that she was very happy to have worked with me in the past and wanted to specifically work with me again. That one project equated to approximately $20,000 and I have been working with this new company (and many of its departments) for several years now."
>
> —Theresa Gonzalez, Stay Visible LLC, New Fairfield, CT https://www.linkedin.com /in/theresagonzalez

- Take a hint from recruiters, who seem to love Inmails: even though you may not target the right person every time with an Inmail, you should add a comment at the end: "if you are not the right person for this opportunity, please feel free to send it along to someone you know who might benefit from it."
- Relieve the Inmail recipient's anxiety: give context about where/ how you met him or her, or who helped you become aware of

---

[11] https://www.linkedin.com/help/linkedin/answer/5868.

him or her, what SEO terms you used to find the recipient in a LinkedIn search. This puts the recipient more at ease and allows him or her the assurance that your intentions are professional.

- And a big one—end with a call to action, why this Inmail is important and needs attention. Perhaps depending on the circumstances, you need to indicate a reasonable time frame for a reply.

In sum, make Inmails compelling, friendly, current, and as short as will get the points across. And of course, since they can be forwarded to others, keep them professional.

Being easily found and accessible is obvious to all, but I am amazed at how completely listing *all* contact details is left out on LinkedIn, to the frustration of the party needing you. Don't send mixed signals inadvertently.

Chapter 24

Halpert's 2% Rule on Recommendations: Proceed Cautiously and Ethically

Let's take an earlier concept I introduced: you say amazing things when you share *why* you do what you do (WYDWYD). Let's add this: recommenders help you best when they reinforce in words *how* you do what you do (HYDWYD).

Now, let's apply Halpert's 2% Rule:

1. Take the number of connections you have.

   Multiply the number of your connections × 98% = those who should like you because you nurture them with WYDWYD, continually blipping on their mental radar screen.

2. The rest?

   Multiply the number of your connections × 2% = those who should love you enough to commit in words and enthusiastically recommend you for a particular situation or anecdote that demonstrated HYDWYD. This is a special group of supporters indeed.

Said a different way, Halpert's Rule says you need to show the number of recommendations on your personal profile equal to 2% × the number of connections you have.

It's that easy but not often used effectively.

Now think of which strong and warm connections comprise this 2% to recommend you. One at a time, go to their LinkedIn profile page, click the three horizontal dots in the icon at the top right near their picture and select "Request a Recommendation".

Now clicking the drop-downs, fill out the form, and the final text box allows you to send a note asking for the recommendation.

Full stop.

Erase the default note LinkedIn recommends. It's boring, not warm, and insincere.

Rewrite it. This is your request to a friend, and it needs to be just right. Think carefully about what you place here. You will likely get a form of it right back in the recommendation. This is where you ask them to recall and recommend you for a certain situation where your yeoman efforts saved the day, greatly reduced expenses, came in under budget and/or early, despite a ridiculously tight schedule, and/or won the deal through your prowess. Give them the bare bones of what you want them to include, and allow them to append some adjectives and comments.

OK, that's the nuts and bolts, and now here's the marketing thought behind this process.

Recommendations, as stated above, reinforce what others say, over top of what you say about yourself. Just as you state your WYDWYD, recommenders layer on top their perception of how well you do it, reliving a story or relating an anecdote that shows the reader in a quick sketch the remarkable work you performed, the capabilities you demonstrated to rise above the rest. They say what you say in a different way and help you make it that much more real.

Most recommendations are general and bland. You can't afford that. Your work wasn't, and what the recommender says about it cannot be either. You want to manage your recommendations so that every laudable attribute you are centering your brand around is adequately covered and accentuated by the right recommender.

But without guidance from you, the recommender does not have the time or creativity to help you paint that picture. So often without your being specific, you get back a general recommendation. The bottom line is that how you get great recommendations is a function of how well you ask for them.

Think of this as an opportunity! You can now get a recommendation from a rather old boss you never got around to collecting one from and reacquaint with that old colleague. They will be happy to hear from you, gratified you asked for their help, and able to retell a story of your great work, with a bit of a refresher or a phone call to sweeten the deal.

Or you can ask for a recommendation in a newer job or project. In fact, whenever I get an email or phone call thanking me for a job well done from a client who hired me, I know the words will fade away into the ether unless I ask them to capture that good feeling and memorialize it in a recommendation. So at the end of the "atta-boy," I ask them to write that into a LinkedIn Recommendation, and I send that LinkedIn Recommendation request online, right away. No time like the present, especially if I capsulize what they just said to me and repeat it back to them:

> *I appreciated your verbal comments on the phone that you were very pleased I was able to bring a diverse crowd of your salespeople with varying LinkedIn fluency to the same end-point in just 90 minutes' training time. Could you please reflect that again in your comments on my recommendation and feel free to add as well any comments your staff made about what they learned? Thanks so much for your business, and I look forward to future collaboration.*

I needed a recommendation stating how well I am able to train a diverse sales staff, so this will be perfect. When the vice president of sales voluntarily mentioned in his debrief phone call the day after my training session that the webinar was perfect for his staff and they are all buzzing about it (true story), I want to memorialize that. The recommendation I actually got back from him was perfect!

Your returned recommendation will likely be very close to what you expect. That's how you can manage the request for a recommendation to the friend and provide valuable insight to the reader in the finished product, reinforcing your brand.

But what if the recommendation is not perfect? That's why writing a rough draft (as discussed above) for the recommender is a smart first step. Perhaps some facts in the recommendation you receive back are out of sync or just plain incorrect and give the wrong impression, counter to what you want to demonstrate. It happens. Yes, there may be overstatements, typos, or grammatical errors, any of which you can send back to the recommender to correct, and then he or she sends the revision back to you. Don't be bashful in asking for a sentence or two to be added in this back-and-forth process to make the recommendation very strong. The person writing, one of your loving 2%, will be happy to. After all, he or she believes in you and wants to make it reflect well on you, and indirectly on him or her.

Once I received back a recommendation that was full of typos and bad grammar. She even spelled my name Marc with a "k" and not a "c." How would that look for both of us? Not too sincere if she spells my name incorrectly. Fortunately, I returned the recommendation to the writer with corrections noted, asked for it to be amended, and she returned it to me for publication. She thanked me for helping her with grammar, a weak spot for her.

Publish it when (and if) you are happy with it. You can only "go to the well" but so many times, so writing a good first draft is even more valuable for that reason. Just don't add it to your profile until you have exhausted all remedies with the recommender. Once published, you cannot edit it (you can only hide or delete it). Once you add it to your profile, it's time to thank them sincerely. You knew that, but often it is overlooked in our busy schedules.

One additional observation that may help you in a pinch someday is that if you already have a recommendation on your profile from a company and you are pitching their direct competitor, you can temporarily hide the first recommendation from everyone, including the first company. That way the other company reading your profile will not see that you have worked with their competitor. Hide the recommendation until you no longer need to, and then "unhide" it.

LinkedIn knows that you did great work in previous positions that wind up to the great work you can do now. Use this as part of the story you want to tell: your experience is an onion, layer on top of layer, the past making the present, the present making the future that much richer.

Without diluting the thrust of Carol Greenwald's chapter (Chapter 37) on ethical considerations for attorneys (and much of the same goes for others facing compliance review), I wanted to outline a few possible scenarios for the language that recommendations can contain. Examples include the following:

- *Good*: "having known Mary for the better part of the past four years stemming from a networking referral, I can attest to her professionalism, honesty and her great deal of industry knowledge. I'm fortunate to have not only done business with her, but call her a friend as well. I am always pleased to recommend her to colleagues."

- *Better*: "i've been working with Risa since first considering incorporating my company. Her wealth of knowledge and experience in my industry have helped me navigate through some rough seas. What I admire best of all, she really makes sure to understand her clients so that she can give the best possible service. For these reasons I enthusiastically recommend Risa."

- *Best*: "when we had significant legal issues at my company that needed to be addressed immediately, Don was the first person we thought to contact, for good reason. He worked directly to personalize a solution to our legal needs. Admirably, he was always prompt, straightforward, and thoughtful about our questions and concerns. He made a real difference in that difficult period."

Chapter 25

Give Recommendations, Please

Here is a way to reward those you value on LinkedIn in a powerful and memorable way: recommend someone without him or her requesting it.

Go ahead, do it! Imagine the surprise and satisfaction on the face of your colleague receiving an admiring LinkedIn recommendation that he or she did not ask for.

However, with all unsolicited gifts there are concerns. They all "fit," just some fit better than others. View your gift of a recommendation from both points of view. While appreciative of this kind gesture, the receiver may not want to, be expected to, or feel compelled to publish it to his or her personal profile right away:

> "Giving unexpected recommendations to clients and vendors is a unique way to surprise and delight. When a recommendation is written about someone who did not ask for it, it allows you to stand apart and become memorable...and folks remember that for a long time. It's a wise investment of time that sets you apart from others and improves your likability!"
>
> —David Fischer, CEO and Founder, Solutions for Growth, South Salem, NY https://www.linkedin.com/in/davidwfischer

- It may be over the top for the ethical considerations in that person's field (law, financial services, etc.) and perhaps the recommender had no idea of the compliance constraints (and potential reprimand) it carries. So be understanding and flexible if asked to rewrite it. As a receiver, be kind and appreciative and find a way to guide the writer to amend it to pass the hurdles you know are required in your field of work.

- Sometimes the unexpected recommendation mirrors a previously published recommendation such that both will be less effective side by side. So a request to rewrite that recommendation along a different slant, highlighting something the receiver has and wants to be expressed by an admirer, will be a better win-win. Your effort to compliment can help in even more meaningful ways with but a few adjustments.

The end result is that mutual respect and the satisfaction that unsolicited recommending without expecting anything in return is laudable.

Just keep in mind the marketing elements that each LinkedIn profile section provides as just one of many opportunities for the receiver to express WYDWYD and the writer to reinforce with his or her recommendation showing HYDWYD. In combination, this effort will make the brand of both parties stronger, visible to all your respective connections in the Home Page recent activity updates. This gains many more eyes for both of you, and a great team effort, leading potentially to referrals or inquiries. Good deed, both of you!

Chapter 26

Effective LinkedIn Groups: Membership and Participation

Where can you find a vibrant collection of like-minded peer professionals all in one place, aggregating around a very specific topic, willing to answer your questions, and asking for your help? They're in LinkedIn Groups.

We all like to think we know most everything about our business area. But sometimes the help of a peer is quite useful. You may need to compare notes, ask a question, or start a conversation in one or more LinkedIn Groups. Why? It builds your network of people to rely on and, conversely, to recognize your name and WYDWYD.

Groups on LinkedIn cover the breadth of human endeavor—from alumni associations to hobbyists, from chambers of commerce to professional associations, and businesspeople involved in every professional and personal interest you can imagine. So it's not just business. It's whatever you do, and you can bring others together to talk about the shared interest.

A Group is closed with the Group's Manager to scrutinize your qualifications to join and probably coming from a cursory review of your Profile. So join carefully and wisely. (LinkedIn allows you to preview the stats for each Group, organized by demographics, seniority, geography, etc., before you join.) Choose to join the number of Groups you can participate in actively. No wallflowers are allowed.

I manage a few Groups on LinkedIn, which means that you have to ask to join and you need to meet certain criteria. When you ask to join, I (as the Group administrative manager) look at your LinkedIn profile to determine if you qualify. Once you have been accepted as a Group member, you are sent a LinkedIn message (cc'd to an email) to advise your entry to my Group.

Often it takes some time for the administrators to catch up with the requests to join, so know that you can ask again after a few weeks.

Once a Group member, you have opened yourself and your now well-written profile to all the Group members to peruse and then inquire from you. Some will be great new contact requests; others perhaps not now, but who knows what the future may bring?

I encourage my Group members to place self-written or curated articles that would help fellow Group members and also to post inquiries that will help them as well.

I like to encourage interaction and conversation on the Group page among Group members.

Group members are not vetted as robustly by the managers as you have done so for your personal LinkedIn connections, so you want to proceed carefully. Exercise some discretion; review the Group member's profile, just like he or she reviewed yours.

If you think there is something for you to gain by answering the questions in the Group, offer your help. If there is more interchange between you and the questioner,

> "When I first started working on my presence on LinkedIn it was suggested to me that I comment on posts frequently in the areas in which I work. One of the first posts I read was written by a member of a Group that I had joined. The discussion was about the use of social media in litigation. I commented on the article, then mentioned in my comment that this is an area about which I lectured and offered to do so for any other members. Another member of that group did contact me—she turned out to be an editor of a journal for an industry to which I would certainly market. After a brief phone conversation, I was asked to write an article for the journal, which was subsequently published. I have since used that article numerous times in my own direct marketing, and as an outline to create a presentation that I have given to multiple clients and prospective clients since."
> —**Tara C. Fappiano, Partner, Havkins Rosenfeld Ritzert & Varriale, LLP, White Plains, NY, https://www.linkedin.com /in/tarafappiano**

you can connect if you feel it is warranted. Sometimes I email the questioner or call him or her to get a better feel before actually connecting. Some have been amazing connections for me and my businesses.

Here's an effective marketing idea: start your own Group, as you see I did in the graphic below. Create a Group of your clients, your informal board of advisors, the entourage of respected close colleagues you rely on. Private Groups such as these are selective—all communications in the Group stay within the Group.

Think about forming a LinkedIn Group for the board of the non-profit you serve on. They are already using LinkedIn anyhow in business, so why not? Boards find these LinkedIn Groups are effective, as they are composed of businesspeople and the communication is more streamlined within LinkedIn than the alternative: a flurry of emails.

Find whatever topic you and the Group can coalesce around. In my case I formed and manage a LinkedIn Group of my private clients so I can share worthwhile and special new LinkedIn-related material with them; they can meet the others in my Group. Relationships developed this way, and I have heard of new business transactions.

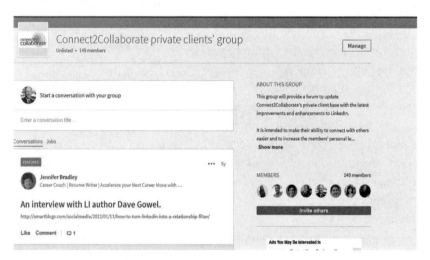

My clients appreciate the educational value of what I and my colleagues post in my private client Groups. That keeps them closer to me and away from the competition. Since I post regularly to my private client Group, I appear on their radar screen, and I can be referred more readily. Yes, this happens a lot.

You can also form a subgroup within a Group. Larger Groups split into special-purpose subgroups to keep the conversations organized along common threads.

Groups are easy to participate in and become a great marketing and networking tool, some Groups more so than others. You can leave one Group or subgroup for another easily.

You can join as many as fifty Groups. Don't. That's too many to be effective. Pick and choose and participate. Find the ones that work, and offer your expertise. Leave the Groups that no longer work for you. Hunt for others. Look at your connections' LinkedIn Groups listed at the bottom of their profiles. Ask them if they get benefit from these Groups and why. In conversations, ask your colleagues what LinkedIn Groups they like.

For consultants, do you need data and insight into new industries that your work is taking you to? Join one or more of those industry Groups and read back through the past few weeks' conversations for background information. Introduce yourself briefly and what you are researching and ask a thoughtful open-ended question for which you need opinions. You may be amazed at what people offer to help you.

These silos of expertise are essentially the best source of current and specific data and opinion you can find. Ask questions in them, and wait for the replies; coddle the Group members for more direct information in a follow-up Group question, if needed. Mine them.

Chapter 27

Your Firm's LinkedIn Company Profile Page: Not Your Website Please

All of what I covered so far is about you, on your personal profile—you, the individual, not your company.

There's another way to brand your company on LinkedIn. Start a separate company profile page to speak about your company's value proposition, contact details, perhaps all your products, services, with a rotating spotlight on one of them.

Please note that this is not the same as your personal profile, *no matter how small the size of your firm.*

A few aspects of the company profile need to be explored:

1. Use a background banner and logo to your company profile page to reinforce your brand and what your firm does visually.
2. Add SEO keywords to the Specialties section on the company profile page template. This will aid in the search for your company by function or other keyword association.
3. Use the right intonation and voice to speak to your audience(s). Concentrate on areas in which your company can help, building your street creds in a very strong way. Use "we" and express what the company can do, which should be different than, yet associated with, what you as an individual say WYDWYD in your personal profile.

4. Create a Showcase Page, a spotlight subpage on your company profile page to demonstrate one of your company's unique products or service offerings. Rotate it as needed (keep a calendar to remind you!) to accentuate a new product or service as it comes on-stream. Or if a product/service needs additional market spotlighting after it has been offered for a while, sometimes repeating it strikes a chord at a more opportune time.

5. Send your LinkedIn connections reminders to visit that company showcase page via status updates and provide the link to the company profile page to get to it easily.

6. Keep it current: don't forget to add press releases, mentions in the press, publications mentioning you or your work in the trade press, etc. Make the company profile an active stage, and show your progress.

7. Finally, add followers of the company profile page. Followers are not connections—no vetting is needed when someone becomes a follower. Be advised your competitors can become company profile page followers, too; company profiles are open forums so nothing should be divulged that you have not already released to the public. By being a follower, they get updates on all news, press releases, jobs, and changes you post to the company profile page, so use this tool effectively to keep them up to date on the latest in your firm; thus, you keep your firm at the top of their minds. Company page followers are not necessarily your connections.

8. Encourage your employees and their connections to follow the news from your company. Invite vendors, clients, customers, former customers, prospects, your LinkedIn connection, and fellow Group members, too.

In my case, I am the sole employee of the firms I started, but each of my companies has its own brand, and I have my own distinct *personal* brand, partially composed of my firms' reputation and additionally with my persona. I have to use my unique voice in each firm, depending on the role and the company from which I am serving the client. Multipreneurship has its definite marketing and branding challenges, and one of its merits comes in the form of the company profile page. So in my case, I have separate company profile pages and an independent personal profile.

In each company page, I assert the voice that will convey *why* to buy from my company on this company profile page. I don't copy-and-paste my website material here. I am speaking to a different audience on LinkedIn (savvy business pros) versus the Internet (the universe), and no one should read the same thing twice. I have an opportunity to speak to a finite audience about the company I developed and work in. And the same goes for my other company profile pages.

If you have employees who have any contact with the business public, be sure the message on their personal profiles and that of the company profile page all are in sync. Do not force them all to be the same or obviously contrived to be that way, but allow their personality differences to rise in how they express themselves, one apart from the others in their own ways, the richness of the company brand as a sum greater than its parts, and this will come across well, only when engineered correctly. Yes, it takes coordination. The public should not be confused by what they see.

Conversely, a single weak link in the company's brand profile chain can create confusion and loss of focus to an attention-deficit reader, so be aware, and review what your employees are saying on their profiles to keep the firm and personal brands on point. It takes coordination, too.

The mission is accomplished only if you feed the company profile page regularly.

Finally, company profile pages require you to establish one person as the administrator with the option of approving managers to help him or her. These people are given the entire power to change your company profile, so choose them carefully. If one leaves the company, sever their capabilities as the admin or managers.

The company profile is a searchable and important aspect of your company brand on LinkedIn. Use it well, and do not let it appear shallow or go stale. It's one of the two parts of your LinkedIn brand.

Chapter 28

LinkedIn Pulse: Communicate with Your Personal Learning Network

LinkedIn not only provides connectivity among businesspeople for the sake of fostering new business, it also provides a wealth of global published material to add to our knowledge base. From there, by sharing great material, as I suggested, we can enhance our collaboration.

Since the wealth of publications is immense, so much so that you can get overwhelmed even when you place limits on it, LinkedIn Pulse curates it for you. With global business pulsating 24×7×366, knowing what others are thinking, saying, and publishing is an essential part of your business life's intellectual work.

LinkedIn provides you customizable access to millions of articles, e-zines, writers, "Influencers" (no coincidence in the use of the "In" part of LinkedIn, identifying influential writers they choose for observations published on LinkedIn), well-received long-form Posts, commentary and otherwise, some established and others nascent, from all corners of the world, on all topics, in all media. Everyone can offer a professional viewpoint, and this is where it is aired.

Too many people ignore Pulse. Rather, you should embrace it as an efficiency tool. Without knowing what its contributors have to say, the points of view on Pulse are all but unknown to you, so in the name of widening your PLN (personal learning network), explore how to properly customize its available information to meet your needs.

Prior to LinkedIn providing Pulse to us all, anyone could subscribe separately to the *Wall Street Journal, The Washington Post, Inc. Magazine,* and *The Chronicle of Philanthropy*, to name a few. Once subscribed, we had to decide how to receive it—snail mail or online—and once received, we needed to be sure to read the publication before the next one comes to us. There were subscription costs, stacks of paper, and the potential for missed articles. Honestly, who today has time to scan each magazine or news edition for articles containing material that is meaningful for today's work?

How do we continually maneuver among the topics we consultants and professional practitioners have to stay on top of at any one time? And how does a time-crunched businessperson manage the topics as they change, and new publications as they come on board, while other older ones may no longer suffice? The volume of daily published material is immense, and growing. What if I miss something? How do I research something most efficiently?

Before Pulse, research was a pinpointed search engine chore, and general reading was relegated to spare time. Today it is no longer that looming, time-consuming task, narrowing the subject matter to only those discrete topic areas and culling the masses of publications to only those we really want to read. The beauty of Pulse is that it provides only the articles that sit at the intersection of the topics you want and the publications you select, at a continuous feed to you 24×7×366.

Pulse updates occur in real time and sit waiting for you to pluck that next article for your education and business use. To make Pulse work best for your specific needs, see LinkedIn's Help Desk instruction guide.[12,13] Select from the dozens of topic channels and wide global array of sources of news for what you need.

You can always make changes later, as required. Now you will receive the information you need most, on the subjects and from the sources you preselected. And the articles await your opening them from your Home Page.

---

[12] https://www.linkedin.com/help/linkedin/answer/56970?query=pulse.
[13] https://www.linkedin.com/help/linkedin/answer/44732.

Once you identify an article that may resonate with a colleague, you can easily share it within LinkedIn. Think of yourself as the curator of only the best material to the great connections you nurture. Everyone appreciates being thought of as the recipient of an article the sender thinks he or she might like. If it is advisable, go beyond that singular colleague and forward the article to a small selected group of colleagues. Or share in an update to a LinkedIn Group's whole interest area because it is probably discussing that topic right now in the Group conversation. Recall that I introduced you to subgroups as good places to share specific interest articles to just them.

Make each share of the material personal: preface it with why you like the article, or where you take exception with the article (it's OK to be critical, professionally), and it's always a nice touch to send a warm note to the recipient saying something like "Jack, I recall our conversation a few days ago and immediately thought you may want to see this, so let's discuss it further over coffee when we meet again next week." Make each touch effective.

Sharing from the best that you have learned in topic areas and from reputable sources is a noble act. It demonstrates your value to your connections while reinforcing WYDWYD (radar goes ping!), and your contribution of recently mined excellent material is the gift of your appreciation and respect.

Chapter 29

Who's Checking You Out; How to Use This Information

I always bristle when someone seems anxious over who is looking at his or her profile. Not everyone is a stalker. If they are just looking, should this be of concern? Or can you use this to your benefit?

To be honest, once in a while I do peruse who is looking at my profile, and if I think there is some possible nexus between us that may lead to my helping them in business, or if I see a familiar face smiling back at me, I will send a friendly Inmail to ask how I can help:

"Hi {name}. I noticed you were looking at my LinkedIn profile recently. Is there something you were looking for that I can help you with?"

Mostly they go unanswered, even though I try to make the contact open ended and friendly.

They seem curious enough to drop by and perhaps read some (hopefully, most) of my profile. To them I would say: if you want to look at my profile, go right ahead. I have nothing to hide. If I put it there, you can certainly have a look. Just let me know if you need my help in any way.

Recall how we said earlier that the public can only see a portion of your profile (your aptly named public profile) and that you also can control further what appears there. Mostly they can find this information about you elsewhere on the Internet anyhow, and that is much harder to control.

But there is one thing I do like to know about people who read my profile: what industries are the viewers of my profile engaged in? To a lesser degree, where are they? That validates to me that I am successfully targeting my brand to the right audience. That data is found by going to your Profile Page. Below your Intro box, a large number appears next to "who's viewed your profile." Click the number to see, at the top of the next screen, the number of profile viewers in the last 90 days.

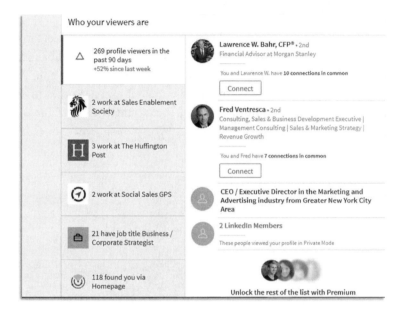

It tells me that in the past ninety days, I am indeed hitting the top four target industries that happen to be on my agenda for more speaking engagements and written works, videos, and podcasts, the media I have been working on and contributing to my PLN.

Next week when I turn my attention more toward law firms and nonprofits for the events I am speaking at and covering on my LinkedIn updates, these industry groupings should look different.

I hope that you will check this analytic often to ensure your industry audience and intended prospects within them are seeing your profile and thus your work as you release it—shared updates, Posts, and so on.

Let's not concentrate on the individuals and who they are, as many are either not going to reply to harmless questions anyway. Rather, let's focus on the broader audiences by industry segment that you really want to reach.

To cap this chapter off, your intent is always to nurture an audience of readers who will recognize your thought leadership in your chosen field(s) and specialty (or specialties), especially where you practice, as well as the ancillary industries that utilize and appreciate your services and insight.

Never forget that the general reader may want more general knowledge, which you can provide, and once confident of your capabilities, may want you to serve as an expert to him or her, or to their entourage and others they impact, or to the people the entourage knows to refer you to. It's a big networking world out there, and your best LinkedIn profiles (personal and company) will help you benefit every time.

Chapter 30

How to Say "No Thanks" to a LinkedIn Connection Request

There are certainly times in our business life to say "no thank you."

Dedication and strong opinion time: to those needy, lonely, not too socially adept businesspeople out there who ask me to connect with them but antisocially use the dry default connection request language: "I'd like to add you to my professional network on LinkedIn." I offer this chapter as a lesson in etiquette.

To my readers, who would never be so dull as to use the default connection request, here's some insight on the best ways to handle it.

In other words, it's a two-way street: what makes you want to be in my professional network, and since you asked, me in yours?

These connection requests come to you via LinkedIn messaging with a copy in your email. In some cases, a photo, name, and Headline might help jog my memory, but not in this case. Since he used the default language to connect to me, I have no recollection who he is—he gave me nothing to go on, no insight or context of where we ever met or how I can help.

To me these staggeringly frequent requests are like you calling me on the phone, and when I say "hello," you say nothing except "hello" back and provide nothing else about what you wanted to accomplish in the call. C'mon, no one does that! No one should do this on LinkedIn either.

My interpretation when I receive this is that a lazy, unmotivated, boiler-plate boring request to connect must come from the same type of person. Why do you start a contact that way?

OK—I'm stepping down off the soapbox.

While my comments may sound snarky, it's because these types of requests to connect come to me multiple times a day, and from people who should know much better, like public relations reps, human resources managers, and other professionals.

LinkedIn gives you, as the recipient of a weak connection request, three choices: accept, ignore, or report them. Thankfully I have only had to report two in my twelve years.

If they give me the minimum to get by and no context to go on, I just click "ignore"; if they start out this way, it doesn't bode well into the future.

One more very important aspect of unsolicited connection requests is that I do not connect to people who identify themselves as a friend of {X} until I check the LinkedIn profiles of both parties first to confirm that they are connected. (It's amazing how many people overstate the relationship.) Then, I look through our mutual connection to the target, and I review his or her profile and decide if a phone call or coffee meeting is worthwhile. In other words, I do not connect with another person on LinkedIn unless I have vetted the target enough to know we have some mutual interests and business prospects.

In some cases, during review of their profile, when I see something interesting, I may reply "Have we met? How can I help you?" to the connection request. There has to be something really interesting to make me want to give them a second chance. There is a two- or three-day window I allow for a reply, and then I make the determination: no reply? I ignore the invitation. (LinkedIn does not send a message to the requester that I ignored him or her.)

If I decide a more informative, professional approach is in order, for whatever subjective reason, I reply by LinkedIn message saying: "thank you for the invitation request. My policy is to only connect to those I have gotten to know well in the scope of my business dealings. I will respectfully decline. Thanks, Marc."

If I want to pursue the invitation, especially when we have been introduced by a mutual colleague, I need to get more comfortable with a new potential connection to ascertain if I should ultimately accept the invitation. A warm referral from a business partner is a great way to (perhaps) start an electronic relationship. Of course, this presumes the mutual connection has also vetted the other party as well. That's not always the case, so I have to rely on my own wits and sensibilities to see if we should proceed.

This is not an absolute. Sometimes there is another motive to connect, although it needs to be teased out from a real-life interchange of LinkedIn messages I had from a connection request I received.

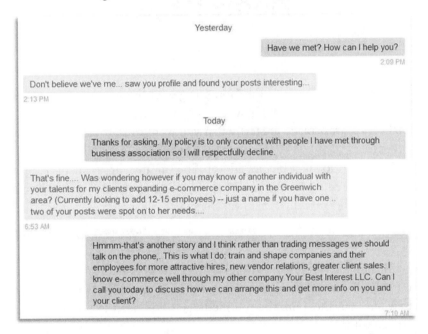

From there, who knows?

Don't be afraid to walk away from a connection request when it seems not meant to be.

By all means, do not connect to someone you do not know or cannot vet. Doing so dilutes the trust and privilege we have in connecting with each other.

Chapter 31

Navigating Your LinkedIn Home Page

LinkedIn packs a lot into the Home Page. As the name indicates, it's where you are taken by default whenever you sign in to LinkedIn. I think it's always a great place to start when you want to start any process on LinkedIn.

First, let's focus a bit on the top line on any LinkedIn page. The "ah-ha" moments I hear when I call my clients' attention to what this line can do for you is always rewarding.

This line is where LinkedIn gives you access to many of the actions you will take most often. Yes, there are other refinements to be found elsewhere, but these are the routine targets you need to become comfortable with.

First a small segue—on the next page, for illustration purposes I have created a composite graphic of the "Me" and the "More" sections you have in the drop-down boxes from the top line.

Note that LinkedIn can change these at any time, and this is often a place the newest iteration of LinkedIn adds or subtracts functions, or reorders them. If yours looks different following publication of this

book, it's no surprise. Maneuver around in this line and its tabs, and find your comfort level by using these tools. Now you know where they lie. At least for now.

The focus of this chapter is the Home Page, opened at top left of the top line (click the Home icon), where you review what others have shared, where you initiate shared updates, new Posts, and so on.

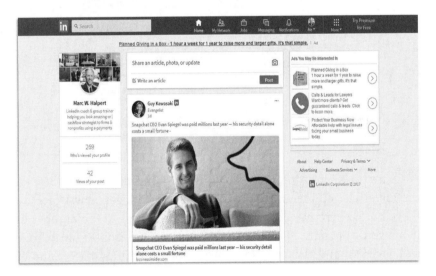

In sum, the Home Page is the communication center to keep up to date with your PLN, and them with you. Get comfortable with all its options.

A couple of marketing pointers are in order to help you keep the contact with your readership:

I find myself looking in my recent Activity (again, found by clicking "x views of this share" on my Profile Page) to determine if my Posts and Shared Updates created conversation by being helpful to my connections: did they "like," comment on, or share them? I get this on a screen that historically reviews what I have recently acted on in LinkedIn.

Here you can see your (and the other commenters') past activity. Hint: LinkedIn doesn't save your material forever, and you can lose access to it after a while.

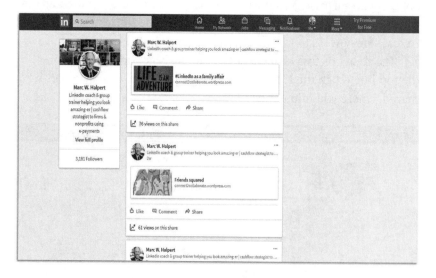

I try to keep a vibrant conversation going around the best of the material I curate and share. Once it is no longer newsworthy, I move on to share newer material. There is no limit to the number of items you can share. Just keep them relevant and important to your audiences(s), and they will be passed along as if they have a life of their own.

Your choices to share material appear below.

Share an Update with the Public

In the first section, you can add a comment telling the public what you are sharing. I let the title speak for itself. All too often all I see is the title and the same words repeated in the comment to the article. Why waste space? Tell us why you chose this article. Do you agree or disagree with the article? Part of your value in LinkedIn is curating material and evaluating it for your readers so they know what you think about it as you share it.

Share with Public and Post to Twitter

While you are at it, do you want to simultaneously tweet it out? If you select to tweet it, you can add hashtags (#) and @ signs to push it along on Twitter, but your simultaneous LinkedIn share/tweet is then limited to 140 characters (including the shortened URL for the article that LinkedIn appends for you).

The Share button allows you to share with everyone on LinkedIn or just your connections. Consider your audiences here. Is it worth sharing with everyone on LinkedIn (more than 467 million as of this writing), or just your personal connections?

Post to Connections

As an alternative, you can also Post to your nurtured audience on LinkedIn connections.

Send a Message to Individuals

Using another tab, once I see material perfect for someone (or a few) I am connected to, and believe it would be valuable to pass it along to my colleague(s), I can select the individual, a few, or share with a selected group of connections. There is a warm feeling when someone realizes you sent along something he or she may be interested in. That's very effective interpersonal marketing that keeps your efforts on their radar so they can refer you should the opportunity come along—another radar ping. I may opt to use this touchpoint as a way to move a project update along and stay top of mind. Why not use every opportunity to capture attention to WYDWYD to your daily work?

Share. What goes around comes around.

Chapter 32

LinkedIn and Your Message: Specifics for Your Industry

Compliance—can't live with it, can't live without it.

I fully understand why compliance and ethics rules, respectively, are needed in the financial and legal professions. It's just the variation among state bar associations and the wide disparity of how financial services firms handle social media and LinkedIn in particular, that makes it confusing for everyone but the gatekeeping compliance officers.

To be clear, comments here about compliance also apply to companies and firms subject to legal and regulatory compliance, but often there is an officer(s) responsible for the company's self-imposed consistency and regularity in social media output by its employees. I understand the role.

I counsel my clients to write only factual, sustainable narratives that never mislead. Do not claim the results you had investing a client's nest egg in the rip-roaring market of the past are repeatable now and in the future, bull or bear market. Don't make someone think you personally can beat the market itself, or that your legal prowess is so far beyond the rest of the others that you can win all challenges and/or cases (more from Carol Greenwald on that in Chapter 37). To do that is just not ethical or professional, in any industry.

But it goes much further: banks and investment houses and most professional practice firms limit employees' creativity in their LinkedIn profiles to the point that it becomes a résumé of factoids and past-looking references, with no value proposition and no street creds to admire—bland, dull, boring.

Additionally, some financial firms have their employees add advisories to their profiles, such as "By joining my network, you consent to the disclosure of your contact information and relationship with XYZ to others on LinkedIn, including employees of XYZ and its affiliates."

This is a self-protective cover over a forewarning.

Some financial services firms are more lenient (well, to a certain extent) and ask their employees to submit their profiles for review. Later, the compliance verdict comes down: changes, questions about wording, stricken sentences or paragraphs, etc. So with time and with perhaps a couple of rounds back and forth with compliance, the final profile is ready, until you want to change it again.

Once perfected, the profile still needs to be kept up to date and vibrant. The challenge is how to know what you can share within compliance limitations. The best solution I have seen is an intranet or in-house computer drive that serves as a library for the firm's employees to use on LinkedIn, containing preapproved commentary material and articles by the firm to share with others.

The problem is that everyone is sharing the same material while trying to stay relevant. It's awfully hard to stand out from the crowd in your firm and outside it with a finite quantity of shared, preapproved material. The roles of legal marketing and social medial management are ever expanding out of sheer necessity, but not in lockstep with the hunger of the employees to share and stand out on LinkedIn.

Yet I sense an evolving tendency to a more open, expansive approach in law, finance, and other compliance-oriented industries. For the fortunate rest of us, unfettered and without compliance officers to answer to, it is important to make your shared material the best and most useful you can on your personal and company profiles, with the goal of helping others.

Chapter 33

The Mighty LinkedIn Help Center

As mentioned, I would never guarantee everything I write today in this book will be exactly where I told you it is tomorrow. LinkedIn is just like that—changing constantly. The functions largely remain the same after a new version is released. The placement of where you go to and access the particular function you want to implement changes from time to time.

I expect that will never stop. Change is good. This creates the need for an ever-expanding body of knowledge you can query at any time, straight from LinkedIn. Most questions you ask the Help Center online find an answer from its body of knowledge or another user whose question was like yours and was answered by other users, and LinkedIn assures it's right. So it's officially correct and monitored.

First, find the Help Center when you click the "Me" tab and find Help Center a few lines underneath your headshot.

Let's research a question I always get in my sessions: "if I disconnect from someone, will LinkedIn notify the member I disconnected?"

The Help Center answer to this question shows user forum questions and answers all around this topic. To the left of the topical article, I was able to click further to a related article entitled "Notifying a Connection of Removal" and found the official answer: "no one is notified when you remove a connection. Your contact information just disappears from their Contacts page. They'll also be removed from your Contacts page."

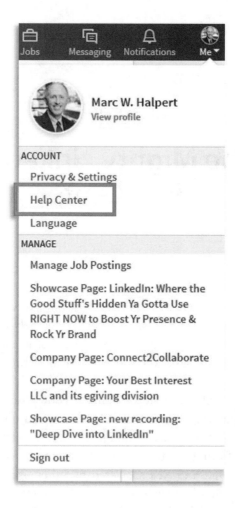

But what if this is not the answer you really need? At the bottom of the page is another way to get the Help Center to dig deeper when the answer is not perfectly helpful. Go to the very bottom in the black field and click "Contact Us" to send a message to start a Help Center case. Then complete as much as you can in the form, and if you can, it's advisable to include a screenshot (as a PDF) to show the staff what you are actually looking at. Expect a reply in twenty-four to thirty-six hours—often sooner. Not bad.

To LinkedIn's credit, they are replying to questions from more than 467 million people within a very short time frame and often using real human language, not machine-generated responses. You get the first name and last initial of a real employee who can help you further. Then if the reply still is not satisfying your needs, escalate it within the case structure. I have never had a case go unresolved for very long. I suggest you become comfortable using the Help Center and all its body of knowledge. It's quite a customer service achievement.

Chapter 34

Considerations on Ways to Connect

We already discussed your need to vet and get to know your connections before you actually extend this opportunity to them on LinkedIn. Excuse me for stressing this again, but it's that important. Connector, beware, as you consider who to approach to connect with. Why? Principally, connections can see all your LinkedIn private profile information and that of your connections. So make connecting to you a privilege, and guard it that way.

Sometimes you find a prospective connection via search, or you come across someone you want to connect with for some shared interest, via a mutual colleague, after a warm meeting face-to-face that pushes the need to connect for the future, and/or other reasons.

It's your choice to offer to connect, given the circumstances, but how do you decide which way is best to initiate the connection request? There are five ways to connect to others on LinkedIn, in either an indirect or a direct way:

1. *Direct connection*: suppose you speak by the phone and get to know the caller well enough to decide to connect to him or her based on what you discussed. You sense it, quickly. You can initiate a connection as a warm invitation by searching for their name and clicking the blue "connect" button below to his headshot, followed by the context needed to help identify you and add your warm message.

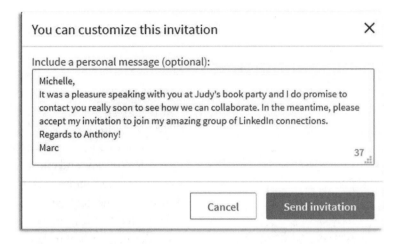

It is advisable to provide context in your invitation, as I cannot assume that Michelle will see my connection request language as soon as I send it. It's me asking her, in my own way of expressing myself. The connection request caps off the call. Anecdotally, I have found that the sooner I receive an acceptance to my connection request, the better are the chances of my landing new business. This is nonscientific—I can't prove it but I do notice a frequently recurring correlation.

2. *Another way to make a direct connection*: you look at someone's profile (via search result or referred to you by another) and see you share a common connection. You should mention that mutual contact you share, and some other comments if you want, in your connection request to "warm" up the acceptance opportunity. Context and good reputations are on the line, so mentioning another colleague gives you immediate credibility to the receiver. (Be sure that both parties know each other and recognize the other's name. A phone call or email to confirm is probably a good idea.)

The takeaway from direct connection requests is that you must provide context and relevance to succeed in your request to connect. It's natural for us in today's Internet age to shirk off connection requests from people whom we cannot immediately place or

"Recently, we decided to reach out through the message function to our connections who are in the healthcare industry. The goal was to let them know in a friendly forum, because we were already connected, about the experience our architectural and interiors firm has had and the clients we have helped. Sure enough, we received a response from one of those connections at a large healthcare facility who had an immediate need to solve a very challenging and serious issue that they had been trying to resolve for years. After a few telephone and email exchanges, they engaged us and we are currently working with them toward bringing about a resolution."
—Marc J. Landow, Landow and Landow Architects, Old Westbury, NY, https://www.linkedin.com/in/marcjlandowaia

identify. And decisions are made quickly, so poor initial impressions can be lasting. Write a warm message to keep the connection aware of what you seek, to make a good first impression, and keep him or her open to working with you once you are connected. It's a good investment of time and effort.

3. *Co-connecting others*: Bob is a great connecter. He is connected to Sandra, a financial consultant, and is sure she will be perfect to help his connection Dan with what he needs for his firm, based on what Sandra just described as her newest service (also reflected on her LinkedIn company profile). That's our guy Bob, always thinking of making strong connections that help others. Bob looks up Dan's profile and clicks the three small dots next to Sandra's headshot and selects "Share profile" and writes a warm, contextual e-intro to Dan and Sandra to draw the two together, providing enough detail for them to take the next steps: (1) review each other's profiles, (2) schedule a meeting or call, and then (3) hopefully form a LinkedIn connection that can result in (4) new business.

Please notice in this example your ability to append a PDF or document to the introduction or to add a URL to the body of the message. If an additional website or a document makes it better understood for one or both parties, add it. In doing so, you have made your point better. This is also you efficiently making the connections, brokered by the admiration and goodwill you have to both people you are introducing. And it makes you memorable as a connector and valuable as a business partner.

4. *Meet in a group*: in Chapter 26 we spoke about Groups as silos of similarly interested people sharing a common belief, interest, or need to help each other revolving around a topic the Group adheres to. In the back-and-forth discussion of topics and issues in the group, some fellow Group members will stand out as especially memorable or admirable. You may not have an easy way to connect to them via another colleague, so why not offer to speak offline from the Group (phone, over coffee, Skype, etc.).

And based on the results of that conversation, ask the other person(s) to connect using one of the above direct connection methods. Certainly end the meeting with a "let's stay in touch" sentiment verbally, and then advise you will follow through with a LinkedIn connection request, in which you mention the context of the meeting and thank him or her for the time and for being a trusted colleague. This is a great way to meet people with similar views and interests as yours, and as Group members they may be closer than third-level connections (strangers). Group memberships can cut through geography, industries, and experience levels, perhaps one of the most egalitarian ways to collect and connect to potential colleagues.

5. *Send an Inmail*: in Chapter 23 we spoke about ways to send Inmail messages to anyone, without a gatekeeper, and sending new connection requests via Inmails is always possible. Beware the viewpoint of the receiver thinking you are coming on too strong, so make your case, show how you can help them and WYDWYD to entice the connection request. Use Inmails expeditiously as they are expensive, related to the LinkedIn premium subscriber rate that each level carries and the number of Inmails they allow.

Finally, I want to make a distinction between connections and followers. With followers, who can see your public LinkedIn profile and/or company profile, you have made no agreement that you share the privilege to see each other's private profile professional material, as is agreed when you are connected. Said a different way, followers can only see your public profile page (what any person with whom you have not connected yet can see when they Google you and click on your LinkedIn profile URL), your Posts, and/or company profile page. Your connections can see your entire private LinkedIn profile in addition to the above. Followers do not have to ask to follow you. They can follow you on their own in admiration of your work. Connections ask for, and are approved for, a connection. There is a big difference.

Choose the best way of contacting and if warranted, connecting with someone. If the person does not answer immediately, a gentle prod may work. If that fails, move on. It wasn't meant to be. Be polite, professional, and expect to continue to cultivate them over time, and vice versa.

Chapter 35

Customize Your Public Profile and Be Amazing-Er

Recall that we spoke about your public profile, seen by anyone, with no connection required. Recognize that anyone can search on their browser for you and see your LinkedIn public profile URL that will appear toward the top of the search results. Go to your own public profile to see what others can see about you.

LinkedIn knows that not everyone wants to show the same quantity of data on their public profile and allows you to customize the data you want the world to know about you. The cynic in me says, well, all of that's on the Internet anyhow, but having had my personal financial data stolen a couple of times, I can certainly be sympathetic to those who worry about their privacy and public access to their data.

When you joined LinkedIn, you began to fill in information about yourself that appears on your two profiles: your private profile (shared as a privilege with your connections) and, with less detail, your public profile.

If you think there is still too much private information there, while signed into LinkedIn, click on "Me" and then choose from the dropdown box and click Privacy and Settings. The next screen is shown on the following page.

Across the top of the page, select the Privacy tab, in the middle, and then select the option Edit your Public Profile below.

Along the right margin of your public profile, under Customize Your Public Profile, you will see two radio buttons: (1) to make your profile

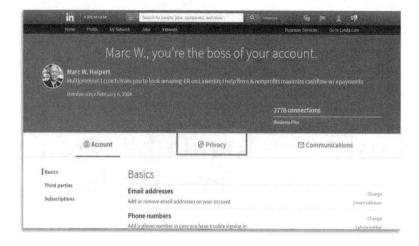

invisible completely, *which I definitely do not advocate,* as it contravenes the purpose of LinkedIn, or (2) to keep your profile visible but allow you to uncheck or recheck the items you want to hide or re-add, as the case may be. If you make any changes to the list, be sure to save those changes.

Those are the mechanics. Now let's speak briefly about why having as much public profile information out in the open, as you can tolerate, is a good idea.

First, a browser search for your name will bring your LinkedIn URL up in the search results if you keep your options open. You may want the person looking at your public profile to see most, if not all, about you to encourage contact as a business prospect.

Second, businesspeople can become suspicious of you when you close down too many aspects of your public profile. As we make decisions within short time frames and with less than perfect information, you do not ever want to miss an opportunity due to an uninformed decision.

I suggest you not set your privacy so tightly that it makes others uncomfortable about you. For example, I encourage you to use your full name in everything you do on LinkedIn. The alternatives for me of being seen as "Business/Corporate Strategist in the Financial Services industry from Greater New York City Area" or "Anonymous LinkedIn Member" will not make others want to know more about me and embrace my unique brand.

Think about others' perceptions of your actions. If you make a change, it can always be changed back if you later find it is too rigid. Just know that the privacy settings are not to be taken lightly and may have unforetold ramifications.

Finally, you want businesspeople to see your profile, to know more about you before they meet you or speak to you on the phone, to know from your own voice WYDWYD, and to read how your past dictates your present and how you see your future based on your present, all important aspects of your personal brand, so they can better get to know and appreciate the real you.

Often I am confronted with people who want to hide their age by leaving out some details. Get past that; they can tell roughly how old you are based on the years you worked. I often encounter people who adamantly refuse to show their photo for the same reasons. Business is about interpersonal relationships we create around us. Do not shut off the emotional or intellectual decision making in your network. Constriction will lead to atrophy.

Rather, open yourself to greater visibility and do not hide anything, unless it's a basic gut fear you have. I am not advocating you reveal your home address, home phone number, birthdate, or other sensitive information. Consider the ramifications of others not knowing some important things about you and how they may affect a business decision to work with you.

With a marketplace aggregating around the global LinkedIn watercooler, you can use your public profile to stimulate more people to want to know you, approach you to connect (after proper vetting of course!), to become partners, clients, vendors, or any role that makes your business brand rock. You may be amazing to yourself and those who know you, but you need to appear better than your competition to those who will appreciate your WYDWYD on your public and private profile (thus you look amazing-er than the rest).

I encourage you to go into the Privacy and Settings options and look around. Each of the horizontal tabs (Account, Privacy, and Communications) on the webpage has multiple sub-options, so there is a lot of room to choose your settings. Get acquainted with the power you have to fully control your image and brand on LinkedIn.

Chapter 36

LinkedIn's Mobile Apps: Be a Go-To Person

LinkedIn can become even more powerful and useful, especially so when you least expect to need it, and then you need it most—when you are out of the office. Perhaps time just did not allow you to prepare fully to know about all the people in the meeting you are entering, or events occurred such that you require some fast, on-the-spot research into a person or company, or you need a quick fact check on the run.

Life has its twists. Schedules change and people pop in and out of your business life. You go away on business or for pleasure. Yet, work continues. Mobile technology makes some of these challenges and uncertainties more manageable, with the power of the Internet and LinkedIn in the palm of your hand.

Indeed, this was the case at a holiday party on a rooftop of a building overlooking the New York City skyline when I met a woman with whom I clicked with immediately, each of us started talking about our WYDWYD, and the business connection was palpable. After about twenty minutes of one-to-one conversation, knowing this was leading in a very positive, professional direction, I excused myself for the restroom and on the way I consulted her LinkedIn profile using my smartphone to ascertain more that I could learn about her to further steer the conversation to mutual interests.

Upon returning to speak to her, I had many more questions to ask her to make the meeting a much more advantageous interchange, helping us delve deeper. When we said good-bye at the end of the event, I invited her to connect to me on LinkedIn as I rode the train back home. She accepted immediately. All of this used wireless mobile technology and reinforced our business relationship.

There is no time like the present to secure a connection and make use of the technology tools we have at our disposal. Why wait until the next day? So much noise and static can get in the way. Seize the moment to make an impression. Then later, feed and nurture those relationships.

Here is an overview of some of the current LinkedIn mobile apps, available on Apple and Android devices. I refer you to LinkedIn's website (https://mobile.linkedin.com/) for more detail.

1. *The LinkedIn app*: a light mobile version of desktop LinkedIn, it has ways to get at much of the same data. It also has definite disadvantages in that not all data is visible on a connection's profile, and in quite a few other ways, but for me as an on-the-go professional, it is an adequate supplement to the desktop version. An idea for you when the mobile LinkedIn app is not perfect: I tap into my desktop from my smartphone, using remote access software, to get to the full array of LinkedIn data I really need while I am on the go. I anticipate more improvements to the mobile functionality and graphic presentation with time. I especially look forward to an exact replication of the desktop version on the mobile screen.

2. *The LinkedIn Groups app*: their mobile service for your Group affiliations on LinkedIn. Following are two ideas for using mobile Groups:

   a. Use this app to read recent questions, answers, and commentary from people in this industry or a special interest group. Honest, open information for research does not come much more pointed than this, so you can use this app to brief yourself on your way to a meeting or for the very latest background in a proposal or talk.

   b. If your business activity is introducing you to an industry you do not know much about, you can follow the discussion on numerous associated Groups to get a broad view of what they are most interested in at the moment. Your street cred rises when you are perceived to know as much about hot topics as the insiders, ask questions of industry participants, and add this new knowledge to your verbal commentary in your sales presentation.

3. *The LinkedIn SlideShare app*: their mobile service to help you read and share recent multimedia material shared by others interested in the same topics as you. The following are two ideas for using mobile SlideShare:

   a. Use this app to review recent presentations shown publicly at conferences, webinars, and so on, from recognized authorities in this industry or interest group. One caveat is that there is reluctance among some speakers to openly share their materials out of concern of material being copied and diluting their brand, myself included. From those who are not concerned about this, you now have their input into your own thought processing for your client, so you can use this app to brief yourself for a meeting or conversation with additional background.

   b. If you are presenting on a topic and a graphic from SlideShare is useful in making your point, you may use it with attribution, assuming the citation is clear that it is not your material. Your slides gain more depth when you bring in other research and expertise from thought leaders to reinforce your assertions.

4. *LinkedIn Learning (formerly Lynda.com)*: the recent acquisition of this online educational seminar service will help you use your spare time beneficially to learn new skills and educate yourself on new topics from experts in the field. Until now, all apps discussed above provide free materials. Lynda.com courses have prices affixed to their descriptions, and there are many courses to choose from. The following are two ideas for using mobile Lynda.com:

   a. Use dead time between appointments and whenever your schedule changes due to last-minute cancellations to learn something, rather than being mired down in email. You can stop and start again.

b. You can also download the courses and watch when you do not have Wi-Fi access. I also see others using bulk time, such as commuting, to learn from Lynda courses.

5. *The LinkedIn Jobs Search app*: this mobile app has dual functionality in that you tell it what positions you are specifically looking for, by search term, title, or location, and it notifies you of new jobs posted on the app that meet your specifications. It is secure and private and very timely when speed of responsiveness to an open position is important and competition is tight. Premium subscription required.

6. *The LinkedIn Lookup app*: this mobile service works when you work in a company that has signed up for this service, and it allows you to search for coworkers and contact them via LinkedIn without using Inmails, even if you've not yet connected to them on LinkedIn. Perhaps not applicable to some of us, it's LinkedIn's way of maneuvering within the company culture to encourage everyone to connect and stay in touch.

7. *The LinkedIn Pulse app*: tailored news delivered to your mobile device continuously on topics and from sources you preselected (See Chapter 28).

There will be different apps along the way. The good news is that LinkedIn took the old giant lumbering app and split it into bite-sized chunks, with specific uses and audiences for each. Now they work better and replicate the desktop experience a bit better. More progress is bound to come, I presume, especially with the Microsoft acquisition.

Chapter 37

Ethical Dos and Don'ts for Attorneys

Carol Schiro Greenwald, Ph.D.

Ethical rules governing any profession trace back to a belief in the importance of upholding appropriate standards. For lawyers this is balanced by a duty to educate the public as to the value of a society governed by laws and to assist individuals interested in learning about and obtaining legal services.

To this end, the American Bar Association (ABA) has provided a set of Model Rules of Professional Conduct, which are continually modified to keep up with an evolving world. All the states, except California, have adopted the basic outline of the Model Rules, but most have embroidered them with their own idiosyncratic admonitions and requirements. For lawyers practicing in multiple states, the patchwork of regulations can create a set of bewildering, conflicting obligations.

This is especially noticeable in the area of social media, because the world of technology is usually two steps ahead of legal profession rules and their interpretations. Lawyers are very comfortable with facts and details, so they have weighed down the basic guidelines with dozens of very detailed, usually restrictive rules.

We discuss those sections from the ABA's Model Rules that are relevant to the use of LinkedIn for the purpose of building a brand, a reputation, and as a platform for connecting with current and future clients. Every attorney also needs to review his or her own state's rules for its take on these rules.

Rule 7.1: Communications Concerning a Lawyer's Services

A lawyer shall not make a false or misleading communication about the lawyer or the lawyer's services. A communication is false or misleading if it contains a material misrepresentation of fact or law, or omits a fact necessary to make the statement considered as a whole not materially misleading.

This is *the* basic rule governing all communications between a lawyer, a law firm, and the public. All other rules assume and build on this basic requirement for honesty and truthfulness.

In practice this means telling the whole truth, qualifiers and all. For example, it would be misleading to say "We win million-dollar verdicts" if there is no mention of lost cases or cases that pay out less money. It also may create an unjustifiable expectation on the part of consumers that they too will have similar results. Similarly, general fee comparisons are usually misleading because it is usually impossible to prove someone is the "cheapest," "the most efficient," or "the best value."

Prudent lawyers will stay away from words like "unsurpassed," "best," "better than," "larger than," "most," "hardest working," "winner," and so on, when writing their LinkedIn profile Intro and Experience sections. If you do include comparisons of any kind, you should document and date them so that a consumer can understand the factual basis for the claim. Most states have added provisions that require a discussion of specific results be accompanied by a reminder that the examples do not represent a promise of success. As an example, in New York, attorneys using case studies need to add, "Prior results do not guarantee a similar outcome."

Rule 7.2: Advertising

(a) Subject to the requirements of Rules 7.1 and 7.3, a lawyer may advertise services through written, recorded or electronic communication, including public media.

Advertising involves an active intention to secure clients. Most states regulate advertising content for tastefulness as well as untruthful content. There are also multiple interpretations as to when information moves from the purely informational to the intentional pursuit of clients.

In terms of approved subject matter, it includes all content relevant on LinkedIn:

- Name, firm name, address, telephone number, email address, website address
- Practice areas
- Base on which fees are determined
- Foreign language ability
- Names of references, and if clients consent, names of clients
- "[O]ther information that might invite the attention of those seeking legal assistance." (Comment 2)

Prudent lawyers will protect themselves by including in LinkedIn's "Advice for contacting [your name]" at the bottom of the personal profile the phrase: "in some states this information is considered attorney advertising."

Most of Rule 7.2 language relates to the referral process.

> *(b) A lawyer shall not give anything of value to a person for recommending the lawyer's services **except that a lawyer may***
> *(1) pay the reasonable costs of advertisements or communications permitted by this Rule;*
> *(2) pay the usual charges of a legal service plan or a not-for-profit or qualified lawyer referral service. A qualified lawyer referral service is a lawyer referral service that has been approved by an appropriate regulatory authority;*

(3) pay for a law practice in accordance with Rule 1.17; and

(4) refer clients to another lawyer or a nonlawyer professional pursuant to an agreement not otherwise prohibited under these Rules that provides for the other person to refer clients or customers to the lawyer, if:

(i) the reciprocal referral agreement is not exclusive, and

(ii) the client is informed of the existence and nature of the agreement.

(c) Any communication made pursuant to this Rule shall include the name and office address of at least one lawyer or law firm responsible for its content.

By permitting referrals, this section validates the purpose of LinkedIn. As Marc says, "LinkedIn is *the* marketing platform for you and your professional practice." It enables you to create relationships that lead to referrals and work.

But are these referrals kosher? Yes, whether you use the paid or free version. In the free version, you are referring LinkedIn contacts and they are referring you just as you would in person. If you subscribe to the paid version, this too is within the ethics rules, because lawyers can pay for advertising communications and can compensate others, in this case LinkedIn, who generate visibility and leads for them.

[A] lawyer may pay others for generating client leads, such as Internet-based client leads, as long as the lead generator does not recommend the lawyer, any payment to the lead generator is consistent with Rules 1.5(e) (division of fees) and 5.4 (professional independence of the lawyer), and the lead generator's communications are consistent with Rule 7.1 (communications concerning a lawyer's services). (Comment 5)

The LinkedIn platform provides opportunities for lawyers to recommend other attorneys as well as other professionals. In addition, lawyers may refer clients to other professionals in a reciprocal arrangement as long as the arrangement is not exclusive and the clients are informed.

Assuming your content is advertising, Rule 7.2(c) requires "Any communication made pursuant to this Rule shall include the name and office address of at least one lawyer or law firm responsible for its content." Make sure to include this information in the contact section of your profile.

Rule 7.3: Solicitation of Clients

> *(a) A lawyer shall not by in-person, live telephone or real-time electronic contact* [e.g. chat room or instant messaging] *solicit professional employment when a significant motive for the lawyer's doing so is the lawyer's pecuniary gain, unless the person contacted:*
> *(1) is a lawyer; or*
> *(2) has a family, close personal, or prior professional relationship with the lawyer.*

The rest of the rule continues to define prohibited and approved direct discussions for the purpose of obtaining work. This does not apply to LinkedIn because members don't speak to each other in real time. In addition, LinkedIn activities should be exempt because connections are made either with people you know or through those connections with people they know.

However, the rule is important because most states have very detailed requirements surrounding solicitation. ABA Model Rule 7.3 Comment (1) defines solicitation as "a targeted communication initiated by the lawyer that is directed to a specific person [or targeted group of people] and that offers to provide . . . legal services." The text in Comment (2) explains that the prohibition is designed to prevent a consumer from feeling intimidated, subject to undue influence, or confused by misleading descriptions of lawyer services.

Rule 7.3(c) requires,

> *Every written, recorded or electronic communication from a lawyer soliciting professional employment from anyone known to be in need of legal services in a particular matter*

shall include the words "Advertising Material" on the out-
side envelope, if any, and at the beginning and ending of any
recorded or electronic communication, unless the recipient of
the communication is a person specified in paragraphs (a)(1)
or (a)(2).

This is a gray area because when you share information without alluding to possible employment, it comes under the professional
responsibility to educate the public about the law. If you append a note
explaining how you can help those affected by the information in the
email or article, then it becomes advertising because the assumption is
that the note is inviting prospects to call you. In that case the words
"attorney advertising" should be prominently displayed on the email
subject line or an envelope for a mailing or the bottom of the written
piece. General information such as personnel or office location changes
is not considered advertising.

Rule 7.4: Communication of Fields of Practice and Specialization

> *(a) A lawyer may communicate the fact that the lawyer does or*
> *does not practice in particular fields of law.*
> *[(b) and (c) omitted]*
> *(d) A lawyer shall not state or imply that a lawyer is certified as*
> *a specialist in a particular field of law, unless:*
> > *(1) the lawyer has been certified as a specialist by an orga-*
> > *nization that has been approved by an appropriate state*
> > *authority or that has been accredited by the American*
> > *Bar Association; and*
> > *(2) the name of the certifying organization is clearly identi-*
> > *fied in the communication.*

Comment (1) points out that lawyers may

> *[I]ndicate areas of practice in communications about the law-*
> *yer's services. If a lawyer practices only in certain fields, or will*

not accept matters except in a specified field or fields, the law-yer is permitted to so indicate.

Thus, the language permits you to be specific in your Profile Intro and Experience Sections concerning what you do and how you do it.

This reflects the Rule 7.1 prohibition against any false or misleading information. For your profile it means stay away from words like "specialist" or "expert." Substitute words like "experienced," "knowledgeable," or "proficient."

The intent of the rule also affects the Skills and Endorsements section of your profile. The implication of Rule 7.4 requires you to check on a regular basis what you have been endorsed for and by whom and remove all endorsements for skills you don't have and all endorsements from people who don't really know what you do. (For steps to modify or remove Skills and Endorsements, see Chapter 19.)

Rule 7.5: Firm Names and Letterheads

(a) A lawyer shall not use a firm name, letterhead or other professional designation that violates Rule 7.1. A trade name may be used by a lawyer in private practice if it does not imply a connection with a government agency or with a public or charitable legal services organization and is not otherwise in violation of Rule 7.1.

Again, Rule 7.1 is the force behind this rule. The name cannot be misleading, imply an ability to always win, or sound as if it is a government agency or nonprofit organization. As the Model Rule is written, it does not impact LinkedIn usage, but many states have added subsequent provisions that could impact language in some sections of your profile. To be ethically safe, please be sure to read your own state's rules.

States' Takes on Model Rules

All states except California have adopted some or all of the Model Rules. California has incorporated pieces of all the ABA Model Rules 7.1 to 7.5 into one omnibus rule: Rule 1-400 Advertising and Solicitation. Most states put their own spin on the Model Rules, creating ethical mazes that confront a modern, business-seeking lawyer with Hobbesian choices.

As an example, below are some New York State modifications that can impact lawyers' use of LinkedIn. We are using New York State as an example because its ethical rules are so detailed as to be impossible to follow literally in some circumstances. The specificity of the rules may cause problems for lawyers practicing in New York plus adjoining states. A good rule of thumb in these cases is to abide by the strictest rule.

New York State Rule 7.1 Advertising

In the Model Rules, this basic proscription to not use false or misleading advertising language is a simple forty-nine-word sentence. For New York State lawyers, the rule adds the word "deceptive" and eighteen explanatory sections, most of which have subsections of their own. Examples of additional detailed requirements precluding specific activities include the following:

- No paid endorsements or testimonials without disclosing that the endorser is being compensated
- No portrayals of a fictitious law firm or a fictitious firm name
- No use of actions to depict fictionalized events or scenes with disclosure of same
- No art that resembles legal documents (all in Rule 7.1(c))
- All advertisements must be pre-approved by a lawyer and a copy retained for a period of no less than three years (Computer-accessed communications, including websites, must be retained for not less than one year.) (Rule 7.1(k))

The rule also contains five subsections detailing what a New York lawyer may say and do (Rule 7.1(b), (d), (e), (q), and (r)). Seventeen comments add examples of material that may be included or must be excluded. In terms of LinkedIn, this section requires lawyers to include these veracity footnotes if they use videos that may otherwise violate Rule 7.1(c).

Solicitation is the second important concept underlying proactive use of LinkedIn's opportunities. New York State's version of Rule 7.3 has nine subsections and nine comments. New York lawyers actively engaged in LinkedIn activities should pay heed to the retention provisions of section (c), which require lawyers to file a copy of the document or audio file with their disciplinary committee and retain the names and addresses of anyone or any group to whom the material was sent for a period of at least three years.

Because each state embroiders the ABA's Model Rules with similar details, it is important for a lawyer to know the rules of any state in which they practice or in which they solicit clients.

A Final Thought

Ethics is a basic presumption embedded in the very notion of professionalism. As such, it is a brand advantage that should be part of your relationships with clients, your relationship with the public, and your business development activities. Be proud of it, show it off, and never publish anything online that you wouldn't want headlined in your hometown newspaper.

––––––––––––––

Carol Schiro Greenwald, Ph.D., is an experienced management and marketing strategist and coach for lawyers and leaders of small and midsize law firms. Her book, Build Your Practice the Logical Way: Maximize Your Client Relationships *(with Steven Skyles-Mulligan), American Bar Association, First Chair Press, 2012, details her client-focused approach to building and growing a law firm and law practice.*

Chapter 38

Pulling It All Together: The Proper Care and Feeding of LinkedIn

Heading down the straightaway, this book is coming to a close. I always end my group training sessions with five extra tips to keep the LinkedIn beast properly fed. There is no rocket science here, and perhaps there is some repetition with these pointers appearing elsewhere in this book, but they are proven tips to keep in mind as you proceed. Each is repeatable daily and should become part of your LinkedIn routine, with the only advisory that it may take time, a little practice, and when you land that first piece of business from LinkedIn, then it becomes infectious. Your competitors don't know these. You now do and will shine beyond them as a result.

Make an Immediate Impression When You Ask Someone to Connect

Do not be lazy; do not use the default greeting "I'd like to add you to my professional network on LinkedIn. Marc W."

This is dull and boilerplate.

Rather, ask people to join your LinkedIn connections like you mean it; use a personalized note such as, "Bob, thank you for the great conversation after today's luncheon about ways we could work with each other.

Later this week I will follow up on the areas we discussed. So first please join my LinkedIn network as we increase each other's connections. Best regards and speak to you soon, Marc."

You can see how I remind him where I met/worked with him. Then I follow up on my promised items to reinforce my reliability and increase the branding of WYDWYD. It's a message I make part of my brand, and it should be reflective of yours, too.

Invest Your LinkedIn Time Wisely

Set aside a certain amount of time each day to "work" LinkedIn, and be consistent in doing this. Manage the time you spend doing this (I use the timer on my smartphone) to share updates, spread great articles I come across, tighten my profile, contribute to my PLN, seek help, and look for connections—all regularly, consistently, professionally, and optimistically. However, don't be tied to just that time if a particularly great article comes across your screen; send it out right away if you can. The immediacy of quality material is appreciated!

Show Your Profile URL in All Marketing Materials

That shortened profile URL is a marker that you care to be complete and use it to point to you in a number of different ways. Include it on your next order of business cards, add it to your letterhead and other printed materials that accompany your name and brand, place it as a footer on your slides and make it stand out on your handouts, append it to your email signature, place it prominently on your résumé (if appropriate), and finally, add it to any aspect of your web presence elsewhere from LinkedIn. Be easy to find and to obtain access to you, and always reinforce the brand of WYDWYD.

Make Your Smartphone an Even Smarter Phone

Download some or all of the improved LinkedIn apps to your mobile device. Now you have access to data and insight into the important people from anywhere. People will look to you as a "go-to" person when you have quick access to vital data on the road. Use it well.

Protect Your LinkedIn Profile Like It Is a Financial Asset

Given ID and password security issues in our electronic media, it is in your own best interest to protect your access to LinkedIn.

Consider using a separate email address that most people do not know to sign onto LinkedIn as an additional precaution. You definitely want to choose a strong alphanumeric (including symbols) password to accompany your login email ID. Change your password frequently as a good practice.

Opt to use two-step verification to log onto LinkedIn: a text message containing a temporary numerical code is sent to you whenever you log onto LinkedIn and it reconfirms the ID and password combination you already have. Think about this safeguard just like you use two-step verification to access your bank account online. Be sure you receive a text message code to open your profile. See more detail about this important precautionary process at https://www.linkedin.com/psettings/two-step-verification.

Never give your ID and password to your admin or a summer intern or a temp. I know so many situations where it took a professional several weeks or months to reclaim his or her LinkedIn access from a nonresponsive former employee, requiring the LinkedIn Help Center to intercede. All the while he or she was without access to LinkedIn. You just cannot afford to relax security on your LinkedIn profile.

Make using LinkedIn and all these various techniques, tips, and options working to keep you informed and visible, branding you as a thought leader in your industry and protected, all at the same time.

Chapter 39

Parting Thoughts to Make You a Greater LinkedIn Success

Take a big breath. You absorbed a lot. I will wager that some of it was new to you: "gee, I didn't know you could do that on LinkedIn" is the common response. Well, now you know what you can do. Actually any LinkedIn book or YouTube video can tell you *what* to do. But my goal, as stated early in this book, is to take you from "who" and "what" to higher, deeper ways of expressing "why" you, and to ask others to complement the "why" with "how."

My other goal was to show you that you can, and you should, use this branding power tool in your marketing toolbox more effectively. You just have to talk about yourself.

That last admonition is the icing on the WYDWYD and HYDWYD that I promised to cover in the Introduction.

OK, these acronyms are the best of all the takeaways in this book, designed to make you a marketing ace. OK, maybe this won't happen immediately, because you always have some profile renovation to do.

Let's acknowledge that it is perfectly admirable to brand market yourself in a finely tuned LinkedIn profile. Talking about yourself is expected. Let's not endure the paralysis of self-branding many people experience.

My point is that if you don't get to renovating, reworking, self-expressing, and rebranding, and do it soon, you will find other things get in the way. There is no time like the present to dig in. And if you don't tell about yourself, someone else will, and it will never be as good as you can say it. Perhaps it will really not reflect well on you at all.

As a result, no one will be apt to refer you if you cannot speak well about yourself. Any (former) resistance to using LinkedIn is so twentieth century. But when you do optimize the WYDWYD on your profile, the referrer is pleased to refer your LinkedIn profile as part of a message to the target. Those warm referrals backed up by your self-expressed values and skills, experience, and past-to-present-to-future vision expressed coherently and amiably go a long, long way.

Make connections or receive new ones; how and to what level depends on your demeanor or how the referrer enabled the two of you to proceed, but do it! When your profile is presented well, LinkedIn makes it easy for the recipient to know you better before the call. They fall in "like" with you on LinkedIn, contact is made, and from that point it is up to you two to make business sparks.

We covered a lot of ground. Now the discussion becomes more philosophical. Let's begin the big wrap-up of all the tips and techniques I have so far suggested to you.

Revamp and improve your LinkedIn profile versus that of a competitor. Ask yourself, "Would you refer yourself to someone?" Be honest in assessing your profile from the mindset of the casual reader. Do you come across as sincere and real as if the reader were hearing you speak directly?

Channel the power of the network: the number of great connections leads to more in-depth relationships. I found that once I passed 500 connections, something wonderful started happening. Others speak of this, too. You can reach 500, but do so at your own pace.

You may be attracted to "movers and shakers." Others will be attracted to you as a smart and engaging LinkedIn partner only if you have a smart and engaging LinkedIn profile. Business can evolve for you using social media as the lever to meet new clients.

As I like to tell the skeptics, work it and work it a lot. The first time you land a piece of business that was attributable in some way to LinkedIn, you will be a believer, just like the people I quoted in the margins of this book.

Make your readers think of you immediately when someone they know voices a need for your services. Reinforce that request with great material so they see you posting frequently with valuable material on their LinkedIn updates.

LinkedIn is a participant sport. Get out and run with the ball. Start with your profile and rewrite it frequently as you change. Life is a journey, and the business challenges we all face need to be communicated, queried, adapted, shared, and questioned among those with whom we are connected. This is not a spectator activity, so if you think that a great profile will bring clients knocking at your door, you are wrong. You have to be in the mix every day.

Reid Hoffman in his excellent book, *The Start-up of You*[14] (a must read!), puts forth the concept of I^{we} in which one person is exponentially more powerful if supported by the connectivity, trust, and referral by those he or she cultivates in the network. The more people you cultivate, the higher the exponent and thus the more valuable you are as a go-to person.

In my experience, this I^{we} concept is so completely on target. I nurture my network every time I use LinkedIn as a power tool to enhance my marketing. I am enriched and empowered by the more than 2,800 (as of this writing) LinkedIn connections I rely on and who rely on me.

Network, share, participate in groups, and introduce good people to one another as the fulcrum to great connectivity among your connections, wisely and judiciously. You may fumble, but pick the ball up again and run farther with it. Your team of connections will cheer you and assist in any way.

Are you ready to get started? Dig into LinkedIn and tell in your best words and graphics Why You Do What You Do.

But don't stop there. Network, share, opine, and press the flesh virtually, and link out in person, too. LinkedIn is but one power tool in your marketing toolbox. So get out of your own way and implement these marketing techniques. And please report back to me your personal successes and business home runs using LinkedIn. Connect to collaborate. (I sort of like that name!)

---

[14] REID HOFFMAN AND BEN CASNOCHA, THE START-UP OF YOU: ADAPT TO THE FUTURE, INVEST IN YOURSELF, AND TRANSFORM YOUR CAREER (2012).

Acknowledgments

First, thank you to Carol Greenwald for introducing me to the ABA, with a special thank you for her contributed chapter, a well-delivered overview of general ethical considerations for attorneys. Please be sure to check with your local bar association for your local ethics rules. However, if you are not an attorney and yet have compliance constraints in your industry, please check with a LinkedIn group of similar practitioners in your field for their advice and counsel, or contact your local association, and/or in-house corporate compliance officers.

Next, thank you to those who contributed their quotes in the book. My request for participation was open ended to see what would be offered, and in most every case, I was very pleased to read of so much success. I tried to provide a wide diversity of quotes from colleagues in all types of professional practices nationwide.

Thanks to Geoff Geertsen for manipulating the screen prints to the right resolution, quickly and efficiently with his usual good nature.

Thanks to the ABA for this opportunity and for the peer-review process that makes this book even more effective and meaningful to the readership I intend it to assist.

And thanks to my wife, daughter, son, clients, and colleagues who I hope were not inconvenienced in any way by my time and attention commitment to the book, all the while being responsive to them.

One more thought: this book is considered to be correct as of this writing. Changes to LinkedIn can, and will, occur without notice. Please know that I have taken every effort to be sure the book is accurate. If you find otherwise, I would appreciate hearing from you to make the next edition that much better and helpful for you.

My only other request from you, reader (other than do everything or as much as you must do consistent with your personality and brand as I showed you above), is to please subscribe to my LinkedIn blog at https://connect2collaborate.wordpress.com/todays-linkedin-nugget/

(a new "nugget" appears every business day) and share my periodic long-form Posts as they are published on LinkedIn to keep up with the latest news and my LinkedIn-related business thoughts. My eyes and ears connect real-life situations to LinkedIn's newest developments and you are free to subscribe to or follow.

I put my branding foremost in my profile and hope you will, too. I exceed expectations; that's why I do what I do.

Why do you do what you do?

Index

A

Abeshouse, David, 45
Acronyms, 42, 76–77
Action verbs, 41–42
Advertising, Model Rules on, 150–152, 155–156
Age (birthdate), 97, 143
Alumni section, 93–95
American Bar Association Model Rules. *See* Model Rules
Analytics icon, 61
Apps, 144–147, 158–159
Articles. *See* Publications
Awards and honors, 81–82

B

Beddall, Jane, 9
Birthdate (age), 97, 143
Boolean search terms, 38–39
Branding. *See* Personal brand marketing
Braunstein, Gene, 7

C

Career, evolution of, 23
Casnocha, Ben, 162
Certification acronyms, 42
Certifications section, 79–80
Clients
    Model Rule on solicitation of, 152–153
    prioritizing responses to, 13–14
    use of LinkedIn by, 8–9
Cohen, Josh, 11
Communication
    of fields of practice, Model Rule on, 153–154
    of lawyer's services, Model Rule on, 149
    via Inmail, 101–102

Companies
    logos of, 65
    Model Rule on names and letterheads of, 154
    profiles of, 47, 115–116
Compliance, 131–132
Connection requests
    initiation of, 136–140
        co-connections, 138–139
        direct, 136–138
        Groups, 139
        Inmail, 140
    personalization of, 157–158
    saying "no thanks" to, 123–125
Connections
    cultivating of, 19–20
    entourage of, 21
    posting to, 130
Contact information, 98–102
Courses, 91–92
Curricula vitae (CV). *See* Résumé

D

Dual professionals
    certifications of, 80
    Headline section for, 52
    Intro section for, 53
    tips for, 51–54

E

Eason, Larry, 23
Education, formal, 93–95
Email, 13–14
Endorsements, 85–88
Essays, posting your own, 59–62
Ethics. *See* Model Rules
Experience section
    company logo in, 65

describing each job in, 64–65
describing gaps in work history
  in, 65
multimedia in, 67, 68–69
vs. résumé, 63–64
SEO keywords in, 64
video in, 48–50

F
Fappiano, Tara C., 111
Firms. *See* Companies
Fischer, David, 108
Fligel, Robert, 15
Followers, *vs.* connections, 140

G
Geertsen, Geoff, 20
Geller, Lois, 9–10
Glusica, Susan, 56
Goldberg, Rob, 18
Gonzalez, Theresa, 101
Google Adwords Keyword Tool, 36
Graphics, 67–69
Grossman, Leslie, 21
Groups. *See also* Organizations section
  connection requests to participant of,
    139
  participation in, 110–112
  starting your own, 112–113
Groups app, 145–146

H
Harris, Joseph, 63
Headline
  action verbs in, 41–42
  colorful and memorable, 43
  effective, 41–42
  ineffective, 40–41
  limited space in, 40
Headshot
  background of photo for, 31,
    32, 33
  importance of, 30
  resistance to using, 30, 143
  sample of, 31

specs for, 32
tips for, 33–34
what to wear for, 32
Help Center, 133–135
Hobbies, 96–97
Hoffman, Reid, 162
Home Page, navigation of, 126–130
Honors and awards, 81–82
HYDWYD (How you do what you do),
  2–3

I
Infographic, 56–57. *See also*
  Multimedia
Inmail, 101–102, 140
Intro section
  company profile *vs.* personal profile
    in, 46
  grabbing attention early in, 47
  multimedia in, 67–68
  sample of, 47
  video in, 48–50
  what to include in, 44–46
Iwe concept, 162

J
Jobs Search app, 147

K
Keywords. *See* SEO keywords
Klein, David O., 60

L
Landow, Marc J., 138
Latz, Jayne, 48
LinkedIn
  ineffective use of, 15
  overcoming resistance to using, 23
  using time wisely when "working,"
    158
LinkedIn Learning, 146–147
LinkedIn URL, 99–100, 158
Logo, company, 65
Lookup app, 147
Lynda.com. *See* LinkedIn Learning

M

Marital status, 97
Marketing. *See* Personal brand marketing
Mobile apps, 144–147
Model Rules
    on advertising, 150–152
    on communications of lawyer's
        services, 149
    overview of, 148
    states' interpretations of, 155–156
Multimedia, 67–69
Multi-preneurs. *See* Dual professionals

N

Networking, old-fashioned ways of, 21
Networking net worth, 20
Nonwork interests, 96–97
Notification, excess, 28

O

Organizations section, 76–78
Outside interests, 95–96

P

Paying it forward, 8
PDFs, 56–57, 138. *See also* Multimedia
Personal brand marketing
    artful science of, 10–11
    importance of, 7–10
    and impressions of you, 14–15
    news ways of, 10
Personal learning network (PLN),
    117–119
Photos, 56–57. *See also* Headshot;
    Multimedia
Political affiliation, 97
Political discourse, 62
Posts, long-form, 59–62
Privacy settings, 98–99, 142–143
Pro bono work, 74–75
Professional experience. *See* Experience
    section
Professionalism, 62, 97
Profiles
    attention-getting, 15–16

company, 114–116
    confusing company profile with
        personal, 46
    creating CV from, 27–28
    customization of, 141–143
    difficulty in starting, 11
    evaluating others', 23–24
    evaluation of your, 18, 27
    outside evaluation of, 28
    ownership and control over, 12, 26
    protection of, 159
    review of other professionals', 17–18,
        100
    sharing edits of, 28–29
    URL of, 99–100, 158
Profile viewers, using data on, 120–122
Publications
    sharing of others', 57, 119
    sharing of your, 70–73
    using Pulse to receive, 117–118
Public profiles. *See* Profiles
Pulse, 117–119
Pulse app, 147

R

Recommendations
    2% rule on, 103–104
    from competing companies, 106
    examples of good, better, and best,
        107
    giving of, 108–109
    guiding recommenders to give great,
        104–106
    how to request, 103
Recruiters, use of LinkedIn by, 26
Referrals of lawyers, Model Rule on,
    150–151
Relationships. *See* Connections
Religious affiliation, 97
Résumé
    dull, drab, and boring, 25
    machine scanning of, 25–26
    vs. profile, 63–64
    using profile to create, 27–28
Roy, Jeanne Boyer, 19

Index

S

Search engine optimization. *See* SEO
keywords
Search feature
Boolean search terms in, 38–39
effective use of, 37–38
stack-ranking in, 36
Self-branding. *See* Personal brand
marketing
Self-definition process, questions to ask
before beginning, 22
SEO keywords
in company profile, 114
in personal profile, 35–39, 64
in Skills section, 83–84
Share section, 128–130
Sharing Profile Edits, 28–29
Showcase Page, 115
Sinek, Simon, 2
Skills section
changing order of skills in, 89
deleting skills in, 88
sample of, 85
SEO keywords in, 83–84
SlideShare app, 146
Social media networking, resistance to,
21–22

Solicitation of clients, Model Rule on,
152–153, 156
Spira, Harvey, 16
Standing out, 15–17
Status updates, 55–58
Stengel, Geri, 99

T

Twitter, 129–130

U

Updates, status, 55–58
URL, profile, 99–100, 158

V

Verbs, action, 41–42
Video
in Experience section, 68–69
in Intro section, 48–50
Volunteer section, 74–75

W

Work history. *See* Experience section
Writing samples, 70–73
WYDWYD (Why you do what you do),
2–3